INSIDE THE
WARPED
MINDS OF MEN

BRYAN AND ERIK JOHNSTON

Johnston, Bryan.
Inside the warped minds of men : a guy's perspective / by
Bryan Johnston and Erik Johnston. -- 1st ed.
p. cm.
Preassigned LCCN: 97-91241
ISBN: 0-9661339-0-0

1. Men--Humor. 2. Man-woman relationships--Humor. 3.
American wit and humor. I. Johnston, Erik. II. Title.

PN6231.M45.J64 1998   818'.5407
                                 QBI97-41492

Published by Swell Guy Books
Portland, OR 97206

Production by Frontier Publishing
Portland, OR 97292

Cover design and production by Martin Kilbourne
Portland, OR

Printed in the United States of America

Thanks to all the friends of ours, whose conversations and actions we secretly took note of to provide material for this fine piece of literature.

Table of Contents

Fair Warning as to What You're About to be Submitted to
(I know you're not suppose to end a sentence with a preposition, but I figured you wouldn't mind.)

When I was younger, and decidedly more foolish, I had this naïve idea that I would someday fathom the mystery that is women: I actually thought that I would understand them. Heh, heh. The things you believe when you're young. Over the years I found that beating myself over the head with an iron pipe achieved the same results as trying to figure women out. In fact, it's actually less painful and a great deal quicker. I offer this alternative to any out there who are still under the misguided idea that they'll find all the pieces to the female puzzle. It's a futile search that will only result in frustration and misery. And, after reading this book, if you still haven't figured that out then I would strongly suggest seeking professional help at the soonest opportunity.

When God threw us together I think he chose the titles *"men and women"* because *"oil and water"* were already taken. Actually oil and water isn't very accurate; men and women can get along, it's just that the interaction tends to be a bit volatile. We're like two unstable chemicals that most scientists dread mixing together because they're not sure if the end result will cure cancer or blow the lab door off its hinges.

As easy as it is to rip on the whole "male/female" interaction thing, there is one positive result: comedy. Maybe that was God's plan all along; he figured life on Earth was just a tad too stale and thought he'd spice things up by making sure men and women didn't quite see eye to eye.

Ol' God's a pretty sharp guy (or "gal" as the case may be), so it wouldn't surprise me a bit if that's what he had up his sleeve from the get go. He threw Adam and Eve together, watched the fireworks and probably thought, *"Hmm. That's pretty funny. I think I'm on to something here."*

In closing, I'd just like to say that there is no doubt in my mind that dinosaurs will make a comeback before we figure each other out. But at least we can go to our graves knowing that however frustrating it may have been, at least we provided a couple of laughs for someone else along the way.

1
Did You Say Men are Hearing Impaired?

Give me a nickel for every time a woman has said that men just don't listen and I could afford to buy hearing aids for the entire male population of this and seventeen other Earth-type planets. (That would be class-M planets, for you Star Trek afficionados.) Actually, this complaint is so popular among women that it's sort of become a sisterhood bonding agent--female epoxy, as it were--a great rallying cry for the feminine masses. If you lined up a million women and asked them what it is that men don't do, you would get a million women giving the same answer: *"Men just don't listen."* As close as I can figure those four words are genetically encoded into all women's DNA when they receive their *chick card.* You see, before each woman is born they must first pass through some sort of cosmic way-station where they receive their standard issue *chick card.* This card allows them to, among other things, change their mind on a whim, buy thirteen pair of black shoes with a maxed-out credit card and micro-annalyze their girlfriend's relationships to death.

Men don't have a *chick card,* because, well, we're men. And besides, we have our own form of literature that binds us together: The *guy handbook.* It outlines necessary guy traits such as belching on command, how to pick your teeth in public and the finer points of irritating women.

Personally, I'm sick of this stupid, "*Men don't listen,*" witch-hunt. Has it ever occurred to you that maybe we just like to act like we're not listening; that maybe we're faking it? Kind of like women and orgasms? Actually, there are several things that can happen when a woman is talking to a man. The first is that the guy will appear to be in rapt attention because he's honestly interested in the woman and knows that all women think guys don't listen. This way she'll think he's not like all men. Ingenious, no? He actually may not be hearing a word she's saying but figures that if he acts like it, that's good enough. There's probably a fair chance he's turning over the pros and cons of a baseball trade he made that afternoon in the company fantasy league, or mentally comparing the virtues of a Big Mac versus a Whopper for his dinner stop on the way home. Women shouldn't be upset by this revelation. I mean, sure it would be nice if he was actually absorbing the information she was divulging, but the fact that he's putting out this much effort to impress her should rate pretty high in itself.

The second thing that can happen is that he *is* listening but isn't giving her his undivided attention. This drives women nuts. When they talk they want the guy to at least appear to be listening, dammit! Actually, guys have this astounding ability to watch a football game, contemplate a beer or any number of things and still retain what is being said to them. . .if they feel like it. I can't tell you how many times I've had a woman say to me, "*You didn't hear a word I said,*" while I sat there, unraveling the mysteries of MTV. It always thoroughly baffled her when I would promptly say, with eyes still fixed on the tube, "*I heard exactly what you said. You're right, Tiffany should dump the guy, spaghetti would be fine and, no, the blue blouse doesn't make you look fat.*"

So what's the third thing that can happen when a woman is talking to a man? You're absolutely right! They don't listen to a damn thing she says. I freely admit, every guy is guilty of this. . . occasionally. However, the ones who make a habit of it are the ones giving the rest of us a bad name. This is where the "Men are dogs" thing comes into play. Women take perverse pleasure in refering to men as dogs, which I have always found sort of humorous because guys don't exactly take that as an insult. Personally, I love dogs. But it's the *dog-guys* that constantly piss women off and get all the attention. And once a woman is pissed-off, look out! You think elephants have good memories? Piss-off a woman and you can expect her to log that bit of treason away for the rest of eternity. You trip little Suzy Portnoy at recess in the third-grade and I can assure you she's gonna have your name burned in her memory until they toss the last shovelful of dirt on her grave.

I appear to be off the track again. No surprise there. Where was I? Oh yes, men minus listening equals dogs. Right. Luckily there are two types of dogs: good dogs and bad dogs. Men who don't listen are bad dogs and may be vilified at will. Men who do typical men stuff that inevitably irritates women, like leaving toilet seats up or not changing their underwear, can also be categorized as dogs. But, these are good dogs, because they don't know any better; they're just being themselves. And you can't fault a dog for being a dog. You just have to make a better effort to train him. And since most women seem to think they can change their man for the better (i.e. train him), then it only seems fair that we should be referred to as dogs. All clear now? Good.

I'm probably letting the cat out of the bag by writing this but I feel it's my civic duty to get this listening thing straightened out. My buddy Yank Pudweller will be particularly hacked-off because it affects him directly. Sorry, Yank.

I was over at Yank's apartment watching the ball game with him when his girlfriend showed up. Not knowing any better, she tried to strike up small-talk with us during a crucial fourth-quarter series. Yank and I didn't even bother exchanging glances; we could read each other's minds. Our thoughts went something like:

"Does she honestly think we're going to bother answering any of her questions until a commercial?"

"Apparently so because she's still talking."

"Guess I'd better do something before she gets pissed."

"Yeah. Hand me a beer while you're at it."

Of course, these thoughts weren't verbalized. Like I said, we'd both been there before and knew the drill. We continued to sit there, our eyes glued to the set. And, oh yes, Yank handed me a beer.

Normally in this situation the guy can do one of two things: He can totally blow-off the girl and continue to watch the game, which of course makes him a bad dog and eventually will land him in the dog house, or, he can toss her a token glance and give some sort of generic answer like, "*uh-huh*," or maybe just nod. I suppose he could turn the game off and hang on her every word but since I don't believe there's been recorded evidence of that ever happening we'll just assume it's not an option. There is one other thing a guy can do in this situation, but it's not recommended. In fact, it's probably the worst thing you can possibly do--even worse than completely ignoring her--and wouldn't you know it, this is exactly what Yank did. He "*whatevered*" her.

She continued to yammer on about the ridiculous cost of azaleas at the local market or something equally innocuous, when Yank just sort of waved his hand in her general direction and said,"Yeah, whatever."

Big mistake.

Her sentence, dealing with some sort of plant fungus that's infecting a high percentage of perennials and therefore driving up nursery prices, stopped cold. As a matter of fact, the entire room went cold. It's like she spontaneously absorbed all the heat in the room and began radiating sub-zero temperatures.

Yank, not the complete fool, realized his folly and glanced fearfully in my general direction, perhaps looking for some sort of help. I had none to give him. Once a guy "*whatevers*" his girlfriend the last place you want to be is between them.

His girlfriend quickly assumed the pose that, according to the *chick card*, all women are supposed to strike in this type of situation. The *guy handbook* describes the pose quite thoroughly so that it can be easily recognized, giving the guy an opportunity to initiate evasive measures, if necessary.

The woman's hands either go to the hips or she folds her arms. If her hands go to the hips, she then will lean forward a little while tapping her foot. If she folds her arms, then she will instead lean back a little bit. Foot-tapping is still recommended. The muscles of the jaw begin tightening to somewhere in the neighborhood of twelve-thousand foot-pounds-per-square-inch. The eyes take on a squint that would make Clint Eastwood feel like a rank amateur, and the lips are pursed tightly enough to turn coal to diamonds. If the pose is struck correctly, the next thing that gets tight is the guy's sphincter. About that time, ol' Yank could have probably cracked walnuts with his butt-cheeks.

This was also about the moment I began making my escape. "Wow, look at the time! Gotta go." I then made a beeline for the door, careful not to make eye contact with Yank's girlfriend for fear of contracting some sort of horrible affliction as a result of her gaze.

The last thing I saw as the door slammed shut behind me was a petrified Yank giving me a glare that seemed to say, "*Coward! Just like a rat deserting a sinking ship!*" I, of course, didn't give it a second thought. You bet I was a rat; a live rat, as compared to Yank, who was about to become a dead duck. Or, in this case, a dead dog; a dead, bad dog. But you can't feel too bad for Yank. He knew the rules. I guess he just didn't listen.

2
Clothes, Credit Cards and the Fear of No Pockets

"*Clothes make the man.*" Yeah, right. Guys take serious stock of their clothing situation about as frequently as solar eclipses. Now and then we'll fiddle with a tie, but more often than not we'll usually just dig something out of the laundry pile and hold it up for the dog to sniff. If he doesn't go into convulsions chances are that's what we'll be wearing that day. Especially on weekends. On Saturdays and Sundays, the average guy will throw on whatever happens to be lying closest to the bed. If the underwear still has a vague cast of white to it, if the jeans aren't capable of standing in the corner by themselves, and if the t-shirt doesn't have more holes than the ones you normally stick your head and arms through, that's your ensemble. And if for some unforeseen reason you need to grab something out of the drawer you've got plenty of time to consider your options because you're not gonna get dressed until noon anyway!

Let's face it, women dress to impress other women. Men dress to avoid being arrested for indecent exposure. There are many things that separate men from women, but clothing is probably the most identifiable. Case in point: Men shop on a bi-annual basis, and only then if it's damn necessary. Women would shop on a bi-daily basis, if their Nordstrom cards weren't about to collapse under the strain. Ever looked at a guy's clothing store credit card? If he even has one, it's clean and unscratched. You could shave in its reflection! A woman's credit card looks like it's been used to jimmy door-locks or start fires! It's dull, worn and full of all sorts of character. Track the life of a woman's credit card and it's like watching the painting of Dorian Grey! You can actually see it age before your very eyes. And if women's credit cards were the same as men's they'd look even worse. What do I mean? Call a credit card office to apply. That boring personal information they ask for is actually just a smoke screen. All they really want to know is if you're male or female. You see, there are actually two types of credit cards floating around. I'll bet you didn't know this! The ones men use are your typical cheap, plastic cards. Women's, however, are made of a high-grade polymer with a kevlar coating developed by a crack team of industrial alchemists. The card's tensile strength is that of NASA heat shields used on the space shuttle, and the gold or silver leaf used on the raised lettering is a futuristic compound tested to withstand even the most unwieldy receipt imprinters. The corporate powers that be aren't dummies; if women used their cards as infrequently as men, theirs would be cheap plastic, too. Of course, you'd think developing these hyper-strong cards would be prohibitively expensive, but then the corporate mucky-mucks are smart enough to realize that any time a woman has to spend time replacing a worn-out credit card is time she can't be spending money!

Actually, it's probably a good thing women use their cards and don't toss cash around like men do. If they did, it would probably throw our nation's delicate economic balance completely out-of-whack. Wall Street would panic, the yen would skyrocket, chaos would shortly ensue, and that nice pair of black pumps that were on sale would get real expensive.

I feel sorry for women when it comes to clothes. They've got all those annoying choices that, I would imagine, make for an extremely stressful time at the mall.

"Let's see, rayon or silk? Hmm, it'll wrinkle a lot. But will I be wearing it to work? No, wait; it looks too much like that new outfit Melanie picked up last week. Oh, here's a nice one. But should I get the taupe or the periwinkle? Oh dear, I don't have shoes that will go with either. I guess I'd better get both outfits and then get a couple of new pair of shoes, too."

I'm sorry, but that doesn't strike me as a terribly pleasant experience. And what's with the stupid colors? Forest? Maize? Cobalt? Whatever happened to green, yellow and blue?

Not too long ago I had the misfortune of having to rustle up a pair of slacks for a wedding, and reluctantly slithered into a nearby clothing establishment. I hadn't taken seven steps when the annoyingly slim sales assistant bounced forward. He had enough gel in his hair that he could have probably split two-by-fours with his cowlick.

"Yes sir, may I help you?"

"*Sir*?" I thought. *"Hmm, what's he after?"* I tried to act indifferent, hoping he might go away.

"Just   browsing.   Thanks   anyway,"   I   lied. Unfortunately, my ploy didn't wash. He just stood there with his well-scrubbed face, capped teeth and tinted contacts.

"That's all right, sir, I'll be right here just in case you find something that catches your eye."

What caught my eye was a baseball bat they had in one of their displays but I figured bloodshed wasn't necessary--yet. I finally gave in and confessed that I needed some pants. That was all the priming he needed. In one fluid motion that defied all natural laws I ever studied in school, he magically gathered up a half-dozen pair of pants and had them proudly displayed before me.

"And what will the gentleman be wearing these for?"

It took a couple of beats to realize this was aimed at me.

"Ah, wedding," I mumbled.

"And what color would the gentleman prefer?"

There he was with that "gentleman" crack again. I began to wonder if it was some sort of ploy to disorient the customers. "I dunno. . .black, I s'pose."

"But wouldn't a nice mauve be more regal?"

"Mauve?" I puzzled.

"Or perhaps a rich eggplant?" he countered.

"None for me," I said. "Never was too partial to purple roughage. B'sides, I'm still full from lunch. Pants 'll do just fine."

This seemed to throw him, so I used the momentary derailment of his train of thought to snatch up a pair of black cords. Two minutes later I was out the door, while gel-boy still pondered my comment about lunch.

It's a simple fact of life that men just aren't as concerned about their looks as women are. And to further illustrate my point let me regale you with an incident I witnessed recently.

I was sitting around with my friend Kristin, making idle conversation, when her roommate walked in. Kristin noticed her lack of socks and asked why she wasn't wearing any.

"They make my ankles look big," her roommate said, matter-of-factly.

If a guy had a .357 Magnum pointed at his head and was told that if he didn't say "*These socks make my ankles look big,*" he would be shot, he wouldn't think twice; he'd take the bullet. Let's face it, the last thing this world needs is guys commenting on how clothes make them look. Do you actually want to hear, "*This ugly baseball hat hides my pathetic, balding head.*" or, "*These low-hanging jeans show my butt-crack.*"? How about, "*This ratty t-shirt makes me look like I just climbed out of a dumpster.*"? I doubt it. The truth just isn't pretty. Of course, that's never stopped a woman. Lines like, "*These pants make me look like an elephant,*" and, "*This blouse make my boobs look flat,*" are standard dialogue in a woman's repertoire.

There's another element to the great clothing mystique that separates men from women, one that, probably more than any other, illustrates the disparity between the sexes.

I was in London, riding the Tube (London's subway system), when I couldn't help but notice the young man across from me digging through his pockets. His girlfriend watched with a look that seemed to say, "*Men are idiots.*" Finally, after a good fifteen-seconds, he found the scrap of paper he'd been diligently rummaging for.

His girlfriend finally spoke. (For your enjoyment please add your own English accent.)

"What would you do if you didn't have any pockets?"

The guy just sort of sat there with a puzzled look on his face while I just sort of sat there with a similar expression.

The girlfriend chimed in again, looking very smug. "You can't even imagine it, can you? You're mortified by the very thought of it."

I don't know about the other guy, but I sure was.

After substantial brow-furrowing the guy finally offered a completely logical question. "Don't all your clothes have pockets?"

At this point his girlfriend let loose with a gale of laughter that all stand-up comedians dream of.

"Are you kidding?" she said between howls, "I've got all sorts of clothes that don't have any pockets."

"No pockets?" I thought. "What kind of sick designer makes clothes without pockets?"

The girl was right. I couldn't even imagine the idea of not having pockets. What a disturbing thought! Where would you stick your hands when you're at a party and you don't know anybody there and don't yet have a drink to carry around? Where would you keep your wallet and keys? Where would you keep your loose change? No pockets! That's absurd! I love my pockets!

The pocket is quite possibly the single most ingenious invention other than perhaps the TV remote! No pockets, indeed.

I suppose that's why women carry purses. Of course, if men didn't have pockets we'd carry purses, too. But then we wouldn't actually call them purses. No guy would be caught dead carrying a purse. He'd carry a bag, or a satchel. Maybe even a pocket-book if worse came to worse. Actually, I think if it were up to men we'd probably call it a "*stronghold*."

"Hey, Bob. Nice stronghold you got there. Is that real vinyl? I really like the camouflage design."

"Thanks, Mike. It blends-in particularly well if I don't wash my shirt for a spell."

I have a theory: Purse makers are behind this whole no-pocket conspiracy. Clothing designers are probably getting kickbacks from purse manufacturers for every line of pocketless clothing they concoct. Bastards.

One time I bought some shorts and didn't realize they didn't have pockets until later that day when I was out on the streets. When I realized I was pocketless, a wave of fear washed over me. I felt queasy and disoriented. Twice I had to wave off potential Good Samaritans who were sure I was experiencing some sort of embolism. There I was, looking like King Geek walking around carrying my wallet and my keys. . .in my hands for crying out loud! In an attempt to clear my head I walked into a convenience store to buy a can of soda, but all that did was make matters worse because then I had to carry my wallet and my keys *and* a can of pop. . . plus thirty-five-cents in change! Oops, I also needed a newspaper for work so I went to the newspaper rack, set my wallet, my keys, the can of soda and thirty five cents in change on the rack, bought my paper and then picked up and carried around my wallet, my keys, a soda, a newspaper and ten-cents in change! Barnum and Bailey would have been impressed. "*Come one, come all! See the incredible pocketless, juggling geek!*" Sixty-percent of my carrying capacity was being utilized as a direct result of some dumb-ass designer who didn't have the common courtesy to sew a couple of flaps of fabric to my shorts. My pocketlessness quickly blackened my mood. I even got so irritable as to have snapped at a little old lady who stopped to ask me for directions. I still feel she overreacted though. I didn't snap that hard. In fact, I hardly broke the skin.

3
The Heavy Discussion

I don't know what it was like anywhere else in the universe but at that moment on my deck it was a glorious sunny day. I casually flipped a dog-eared page in the very guy-like action novel I was reading while a gentle breeze licked at my naked toes.

All was right with the world.

It was a shame that not everyone was having the same spectacular afternoon I was partaking in. . .as I soon discovered.

I'd reached a crucial part in the book where the brazen hero was in imminent peril. Death would have been certain, except that he'd just fashioned a conveniently effective diversionary tactic through the use of a Zippo lighter, a cheap Bic pen and a box of cherry

Pop-Tarts. Right about the time where the villains were cursing their luck and vowing not to underestimate their foe in the future, a sudden chill crept up my spine. Annoyed, I set aside my book and swept my gaze across the sky to see if maybe a wayward cloud had temporarily obstructed Mr. Sun. Upon seeing not as much as a wiff of cloud I licked my finger and held it aloft, checking for a sudden breeze. My finger remained warm and damp. The air was still as a tomb, which is exactly what I felt like I was suddenly in. A certain uneasiness began making it's way through my central nervous system.

As this slow dread began to form in the mushy, grey part of my brain I heard the telltale sounds of the screen door squeak open. Upon turning to see my roommate amble through I immediately knew what was sending out this "gloom-vibe." Something was most definitely up. My roommate, normally a proud, strong man--a "guy" in the truest sense of the word--looked like a whipped dog. An ashen pallor had taken up residence on his face and his shoulders had the unmistakable slump of a man who's looked into the abyss and didn't particularly like what he saw. He collapsed into the fold-out beach chair next to me and began studying the fibrous wood-grain of the deck.

The cold frustration radiating from my roomie obliterated my glorious sunny day and I knew that the only way I'd get to the next chapter in my book was to find out what was raining on his parade, cheer him up and get him the heck out of there. Although it didn't take the amazing Kreskin to see what was on his mind. He was plainly afflicted with man's most common malady.

"Chicks," he mumbled glumly, slowly shaking his head.

I immediately saw that he wasn't just frustrated, he was bugged. When guys are frustrated with women we'll usually just hang our head and say with a heave of resignment, "*women.*" But when we're bugged, women become "*chicks.*" I don't suppose I have to go into the colorful list of labels women take on when we're flat out pissed. Actually it's probably not much longer than the same list women have for men.

Upon hearing "*chicks*" I took this as my signal to get beer. I could see this was going to be one of those talks where guys will sit around lamenting the fact that women make absolutely no sense whatsoever. These discussions can only be made over beer. Don't ask me why, it's just another unwritten rule in the *guy handbook*. (All rules in the *guy handbook* are unwritten. If they were written it would probably be in guy-fashion which means really lousy grammar and poor penmanship, and we'd never be able to make heads or tails of what we're reading.)

We guys seem to have a fair amount of these unwritten rules but I think that just ties in with our sports upbringing. There are hundreds of unwritten rules in sports. They're not in any book, but you grow up learning them anyway. Like, "*Never make the last out at third base.*" In this case it's "*Always discuss women problems over beer.*" It can be really cheap beer, too. In fact, it's encouraged. You feel kind of foolish lamenting your general lack of knowledge about women over a Hefeweisen, but trashing women with a bottle of Oly in your grip looks a lot more guy-like. Plus, it just feels good in your hand, and gives you a sense of security. Sort of like a blanky that makes you burp.

It was readily apparent what was on his mind. He'd been dating the same girl now for about three months and it was about time she and he had "*one of those talks.*" You see, there are two phrases that strike fear into the hearts of men. Not surprisingly, it's women who have the patent on these phrases. It's true. I checked in the library of congress. The two phrases are, "*We need to talk*" and, "*Where is this relationship going?*" And the funny thing is, women love to pose these phrases to men at the worst possible times. Usually around one in the morning. What's up with that? This is a greater mystery than the great pyramid of Egypt. For trying to plumb the depths of such a mystery you'd think I could receive grant money for research. Ha! Fat chance. Somewhere along the bureaucratic chain of trying to get funding one of the people signing-off on the financing would most assuredly be a woman, and don't tell me a woman is going to make getting an answer to this question any easier. Discovering truths to questions such as this must be hard won, and the bond of sisterhood is much too strong. I can see her now: Armani suit, classic features, leaning back into her deep leather chair, an impish grin slowly curling her lips, as she reaches for the gold-plated Zippo for just these situations. The last thought crossing her mind as she watches the grant application immolating in the ash tray. . . "*Nice try, sucker.*"

Maybe women wanting to talk relationship stuff with guys in the waning hours of the night is one of *their* unwritten rules. Although I have my suspicions that it's more of a strategy and tactics thing, but I'll get to that later.

First, let's get back to those two pesky phrases and try to break them down to their basic components. Let's start with "*We need to talk.*" Also know to men as the *kiss of death*. A guy hears this phrase and a bead of sweat spontaneously forms on his brow. The typical body-english would be as follows: guy's eyes begin flashing around, desperately looking for a diversionary tactic or quick escape. Failing to find something easily ignitable that would create a goodly amount of smoke, he'll then fall back into a defensive posture. After watching countless war movies, guys have figured that if escape is impossible, regroup, take the high ground and attempt to wait out the opponent. This is also known as stalling for time. You never know when a convenient power outage might happen along, providing you with the perfect opportunity to slink away in the confusion. Guys aren't picky when it comes to excuses to get out of this conversation.

Next, the guy will cross his arms, lean back and say something innocent like, "*Ok, so what do you want to talk about?*" This is another thinly veiled stall. She knows damn well that you know what she wants to talk about but you're not about to make this situation any easier. The woman at this time will counter the man's leaning back by leaning forward. I would assume this is to try to show the guy she's really concerned, but we're not buying it. It's always kind of entertaining being in a bar or restaurant late at night and seeing a couple having one of these discussions. You don't even have to hear what's being said, you can can just tell by the body language that another poor sap is being herded into "*the discussion.*" You'd think by now that we guys would always carry some kind of diversionary device with us whereever we go so that even if we don't need it ourselves it will always be on hand if we see another guy in a desperate situation. Of course, that's the theory. Here's the practice. . .

One time while trapped in such a moment, in my search for escape I glanced around the restaurant and saw that at least four other guys recognized my plight but weren't doing a thing to help me. I figured at least one of them would have had the decency to affect a drunken stupor and trip over our table or something, providing me with an out, but no. I shouldn't be too surprised though. Getting between a guy and his girl when they're having "*the heavy discussion*" is like getting between a guy and his girl after he "*whatevered*" her. It's just not something you want to do.

Ok, let's move along. The phrase, "*We need to talk,*" is usually followed by something along the lines of, "*You've been acting differently lately,*" or "*I'm getting weird vibes from you.*" Chances are, you're right, but the standard guy response should always be, "*I don't know what you're talking about. Everything's cool.*" This is a flagrant lie but according to the *guy handbook* it's standard operating procedure, and no guy wants to be the one to break tradition. It's about this time where guys pull the old ostrich bit. It's childish but effective. There's another unwritten rule in the *guy handbook* that says, "*Ignore the problem and it will go away.*" Now, every guy knows this is a bunch of crap, but it is, after all, an unwritten rule so who are we to challenge it? We may not be able to communicate worth a damn but never let it be said that men aren't bound by principles of honor. And recognizing the time-honored tradition of ignoring a problem is a principle that all men shall be held to.

Now, the second phrase: "*Where is this relationship going?*" is frequently just a sub-text of the much more encompassing, "*We need to talk.*" If the woman is feeling charitable she'll often lead with "*We need to talk*" and promptly follow with "*Where is this relationship going?*" This way, instead of setting up two separate, uncomfortable discussions, she lets you have both barrels at once. Very few men have walked away from the twin killers unscathed. It is, however, a double-edged sword. If she only poses one of the two phrases there's always a chance you can BS your way through. But at the same time you know full-well she still has one shell left in the chamber, and she's just biding her time to cock the hammer a second time. There isn't enough BS in most guy's repertoire to withstand both barrels at once. Sooner or later we cave in and cough up secret information. Perhaps this is why women hit us with these discussions in the wee hours of the morning. We're tired and vulnerable. The last thing in the world we want to discuss is relationship stuff. Women aren't dummies. They sense this, like fear, and pounce on it like a starving dog on a pork chop. They know they'll outlast the guy in a relationship discussion and are bent on winning by way of attrition. Now, that right there has got to be some kind of weird genetic thing. A woman can go dancing all night, drink seven beers and be exhausted at the end of the night. . .until she wants to talk about the relationship. All of a sudden she's copped a second, third and fourth wind, and we're just about down for the count. If scientists can isolate this energy gene who knows how many viruses would soon fall?

If you'll recall a few paragraphs earlier I was talking about how women probably figure they won't come out of the discussion empty-handed if only they start late at night and wait the guy out. Here's where my strategy and tactics theory comes into play. There are high-paid military geniuses at the pentagon who honestly don't think women would make good field commanders. Ha! Patton should have been so cagey. These military pundits have obviously never been caught in a relationship discussion with a woman. If, in the heavy relationship discussion, a woman can't get everything she wants out of the guy, she'll wear him down. If Hitler had the patience that women have, we'd all be eating bratwurst and weinerschnitzel right now. Sooner or later the man is gonna cave in and give up something just to make the woman happy so he can go to sleep. This is known as "*relationship plea-bargaining*," and for most guys is an expected and acceptable way out of the discussion. I've plea-bargained relationship info more times than I can remember. So what happens if you don't plea-bargain? Chances are she's gonna throw the book at you. . . as well as a couple of vases and lamps, too.

4
Talk, Discuss, Solve and Ignore

Let's cut to the chase. Women's favorite topic of discussion is men. OK, they may not talk about men more than any other subject, but their male-oriented conversations are much more indepth, heated and colorful. Men's favorite topic of discussion, however, is sports. This explains a great deal about why men and women are seldom on the same wavelength and why relationships are such tenuous things. They're really one-sided in the concentration department. Women simply dwell on them more than men do--especially when they're in the middle of one. They're analyzing the relationship, what's working, what's not; trying to fathom that which is fathomless. Guys, on the other hand, are thinking "*If it ain't broke, don't fix it.*" Of course, we also have a tendency to think "*Even if it is broke, it'll probably fix itself anyway.*" (See "ignore the problem.")

It's this astounding ability to concentrate on one subject that makes me think that not only are women outstanding strategists like I'd discussed in the previous chapter, but that all women are born scientists as well. They'll focus on something and analyze it to death. There's always some hidden meaning, a secret agenda. If we could harness the energy women put into understanding relationships and direct it toward discovering a cure for cancer, chemotherapy would be a thing of the past. I wish I had the ability to focus on something like a woman does on a relationship. It's nothing short of miraculous. Right now, I'm taking a foreign language; Norwegian, if you must know. I've always kind of sucked when it comes to learning a foreign language, because I find myself getting bored exceedingly fast. (Imagine, a guy quickly getting bored with something.) My attention span has a hard enough time in English. Now, the way I figure it, if I could somehow corral that focusing ability that's hiding somewhere in the feminine quadrant of my psyche, I'd ace Norwegian. Right now when I look at a lengthy sentence in Norwegian, I see a confusing list of words. If I could look at it like a woman looks at a relationship I could instantly break down the sentence structure and clear things right up.

"*Let's see, here's the noun. What's the noun doing there? Oh, there's the verb. Maybe now I can see what that noun's got on it's mind. And where's that pesky adjective? Oh, so that's how the noun is going to be, is it?"*

Suddenly the sentence has been pinned down, peeled open and inspected like a frog in science class. I don't have this analytical chromosome. And come to think of it, with this obviously advanced gene, there's no reason women should get anything but A's in school.

Maybe this analyzing ability isn't a genetic thing after all. Maybe it's something that everyone has, but like a muscle it must be used or it atrophies. That would explain a lot. With the amount of use women put it to, over the years they've pumped it up to Schwarzennegerian proportions. Whereas, guys have sort of ignored that muscle, and as a result, when looking at relationships we take on the emotional dimension of the guy in the Charles Atlas ads in the back of comic books who gets sand kicked in his face.

One time when I was hanging out with my friend Tammy I casually mentioned that I'd seen my buddy Jay over the weekend. The questions then came hurtling at me at a staggering pace.

First she peppered me with the simple stuff.

"Oh, I love Jay! How is he?" she peppered.

"He's fine." I said.

"Is he seeing anybody?"

"Beats me. Didn't ask."

Tammy then gave me the kind of look most women give men when they'd like to smack them in the side of the head but are afraid they might do more damage than is already apparent, so they just give the look instead.

"Whattaya mean you didn't ask?"

"I didn't ask. What's the problem? I didn't figure it was any of my business," I answered back with no less than a trace of irritability.

Not asking one of my friends I hadn't seen in a while if he was dating anyone was such an alien idea to Tammy that she was rendered mute for at least a good thirty seconds. Her jaw just kind of hung there in stunned silence as she tried to process my very guy-like response.

Let's face it, people like to talk about what they know, and women know relationships. Do you know how much guys talk about relationship stuff with their buddies? I'll give you a hint, relationship talk doesn't hold a candle to a good baseball box-score discussion. Occasionally, when something big is going on, like he just met somebody he's really excited about or his girlfriend just freaked out, then he'll talk with his buddies over a beer. But more often than not, he won't.

Here is a typical discussion between two guys after one of them just had a first date.

Guy 1: So how'd it go last night?

Guy 2: Went fine.

Guy 1: Cool. Any potential?

Guy 2: Maybe. She's a Mariners fan.

Guy 1: No shit? Gotta love that. Hey, did you happen to catch the game last night?

That's it. Sure, if you're feeling particularly saucy, and if you've had a couple of beers, you're bound to ask the question, "*Any action*?" Usually, though, you save that one for later. Now, let's go back to that same discussion but between two women.

Woman 1: So how'd it go last night?

Woman 2: It went fine. (At this point the similarities between the men's discussion and the women's ends.)

Woman 1: What did you wear?

Woman 2: I wore jeans with my white blouse and that new red blazer I got at Nordstroms for Christmas.

Woman 1: Oh, that one looks so good on you. Did you wear those black pumps, the ones with the little leather strap on top? I love those.

Woman 2: Thanks. Do you wanna borrow them sometime?

Woman 1: Sure! So, where did you go?

And that's only the clothing part of the conversation. There's still the dissection of the guy's character, taste in clothes, manners, etc. I could go on but this discussion alone would take up thirty pages in itself. Women can discuss a date endlessly. There's no detail too small, no gesture too obscure. They want to know times, dates, car make and model, metric weight, molecular density, etc. And in these discussions, women can be so much more crude than men. Guys may ask flat out if you got laid last night, but don't normally need a lot of details. Women may not ask in so many words, they might just initiate the conversation by saying something like, "So. . . anything _interesting_ happen?" At which point all bets are off. If that poor guy has as much as an embarrassing birthmark, you can rest assured that by the next evening half a dozen other women are gonna know about it. Women will ask every question in the book and the astounding thing is that the woman being asked will usually cough up the information. Is nothing sacred?

The ability to discuss something, ad nauseum, is just another of the great differentiators between men and women. One time, I happened to visit some female friends of mine the day after one of them had a serious knock-down, drag-out with her boyfriend. She went on and on about how she was sure it was over, how pissed he was, what she did wrong, how he overreacted, ya-de-ya-de-ya-de-ya. I did my best to lend an understanding ear and was surprised when I glanced over at one of her roommates to see not the least bit of empathy registering on her face. Actually, what I saw was rolling of eyes, tapping of fingers and other physical expressions that bear the signature of impatience.

I listened attentively and when she asked my opinion I offered a guy's perspective and tried to help her get some answers to her dilemma. What was I thinking? Help her get some answers? She didn't want answers, she just wanted to talk about it.

Give a guy a problem and the last thing he wants to do is talk about it. He either wants to ignore it completely or roll up his sleeves, find an answer, fix it and get it out of the way. Give a woman a problem and she wants to discuss it--indefinitely--preferably over wine.

I can hear you women readers now, "*Guys fix a problem? You even mention problems with the relationship and they run for cover.*"

Fair enough. But relationship stuff doesn't constitute a problem, per say. Trying to fit a carburetor from '77 Impala into a Ford Fiesta, now that's a problem. Figuring out how to get more run production out of the bottom half of your softball team's batting order would also be worthy of serious consideration. But relationship stuff? That's too nebulous. It has no substance, no physical proportions. It's like a black hole. Mathematics proves they exist but no one's ever seen one. If a guy can't get his hands around it, get a socket wrench on it, kick it with his Doc Martins, or look at it from three different sides, it doesn't register on the problem scale; and therefore is relegated to the long list of "*to be ignored.*"

Another sidebar to the "*discuss vs. solve,*" dilemma is what I like to call the "*fret factor.*" Fretting comes from *looking* at a problem too long. Fretting comes from *discussing* a problem too long. Fretting comes from over-zealous *analyzation* of a problem. In short, women fret more than men. Some women would say that men have a neanderthal mentality about dealing with a problem if they can't get it solved immediately. I disagree. I like to think of how we handle these situations as "*efficient.*" What do we do, and how do we get our fret factor so low as to barely register on the fret scale? It's actually quite simple. We'll usually just sort of knit our brow, place our hands firmly on hips and say. . ."*Screw it. I'll worry about it later.*"

Women don't say "*screw it,*" nearly enough. Saying "*screw it,*" can derive amazing results. "*Screw it,*" has been know to render the fret factor to almost nil. "*Screw-it,*" relieves stress. "*Screw it,*" leaves you plenty of time to play golf. "*Screw it,*" is man's wonder drug.

Case in point: Once I walked in on my mom, who was obviously in a deep fret over something.

"What are you fretting about, Mom?"

She just sort of stood there, twirling a tuft of hair with her index finger and fretted some more. "We've got twenty-five guests coming over next week and I can't, for the life of me, figure out how to rearrange the furniture to make sure there's plenty of room for everyone."

I looked around the room for a moment, quickly determined the options available and offered them up. She didn't budge. She just kept twirling and fretting.

"I just don't know," she muttered.

I knew better than to offer shifting the furniture around because she'd only change her mind after I'd successfully ruptured three discs and discovered that a sudden hernia had forced my spleen to migrate to the opposite side of my abdomen.

"I just don't know," she muttered some more.

At this point I went to the well for that golden nectar that relieves all frets. "Ah, Mom, screw it. Worry about it later."

In my eyes the problem was dealt with in a clean and efficient manner until some later date too far into the future for me to contemplate. Upon feeling my own minor stress instantaneously melt away I turned to go find something to fiddle with. My mom, of course, still stood there with an even larger look of fret spread across her face. I half expected a flock of pigeons to take up roost on her head, with the amazing stillness she'd achieved. Fretting has a way of doing that-immobilization. I briefly considered trying to shake her out of it but then thought *"Ah, screw it."* Amazing. I felt better already.

5
Why Cats Hang Out with Dogs

How many times have women heard the immortal words, "*trust me,*" from a guy? An unscientific phone survey by the authors of this book determined the number to be somewhere between thirty-eight and thirty-nine bajillion, give or take. In other words, more times than there are grains of sand on the combined beaches, and deserts of the world—and any other worlds for that matter. Needless to say, our phone bill was on the high side that month.

Let's face it, guys have never really given women too many reasons to trust them. We say, "*I'll call you,*" and don't. We say, "*I'll write every day,*" and don't. Our track record in the trust department isn't exactly exemplary, so why is it that it seems most women have more guy-friends than gal-friends? What ever happened to the almighty bond of sisterhood? I've got a hunch that women trust other women even less than they trust us guys. So if they won't trust men as far as they can throw them and trust women even less, who's left?

Maybe it's a competition thing? Guys by nature are very competitive. That explains why the male ego is such a fragile thing. But we don't seem to be as competitive about women as we are about sports stuff. I know that sounds ludicrous so let me qualify it. If it's fourth and goal, I'll be damned if I'm gonna let my guy score on me. In this situation it's him against me. There are no other factors involved. But when the competition is over a woman, things change. Suddenly there are extraneous factors, like the woman's taste in men. Sure, if there are two of us going for the same girl, I can assure you we're both gonna go at her hell-bent on election, but as soon as one guy sees the girl appears more interested in the other guy, he backs off. For one, you can always write it off that the woman wouldn't know a classy guy if he came up and bit her on the butt. How can you possibly win in a situation where the judge's sensibilities are so completely out of whack? In other words, it's easy to rationalize yourself into feeling better about losing out.

The second reason, and the more important reason, is that it's unwritten rule number seventy-three: *You don't mess with another man's woman.* Unless you fall into the *"bad dog"* category, which we discussed earlier. Women, however, aren't as prone to follow unwritten rule number seventy three. Maybe it's just me, but I think that once a woman sets her mind on getting a guy, thoughts of a charging bull rhino come to mind. Women don't let a lot stand in their way.

I remember a time when a couple of buddies and I were out, partaking of the fine malted beverages of one of our town's classier drinking establishments; "*Moe's pit*," if I recall. My buddy Bruce had a date in tow, which struck me as a particularly crass move on his part. If she was his girlfriend, cool. But we were drinking, and she was an outsider. Besides, she was good looking and we couldn't hit on her. (See unwritten rule number seventy three.) Now, my buddy Bruce falls into the category of *studly dude*. Women dig Bruce. And to top it off, he compounds the issue by being an annoyingly good guy. This abhorrent combination of looks and charm has more than once dealt ruthian blows to my already fragile male ego. On at least seven separate occasions playboy-esque goddesses have conveniently bumped into me, struck up sincere conversations, and even tossed in a couple of good token guffaws at my tasteless jokes before dropping the bomb on me: "*Is your friend single?*" For all the times Bruce has inadvertently dashed my hopes, it's a wonder I haven't hired a couple of goons to kneecap him.

At any rate, here we are swilling beer and enjoying a pleasant evening rendition of, "*I've had more stitches than you;*" always a guy favorite. My buddy's date couldn't seem to fathom the entertainment value of our contest but gamely endured our painfully descriptive stories. I have to hand it to her, she hung in there admirably until my pal "*Three-fingered Swede*" told us why he had to change his name *from* "*Four-fingered Swede*" to his current moniker.

"Hey, Bruce," I offered, "this one's got potential. She made it all the way through the part about The Swede's mishap with the ice-axe before bolting for the bathroom."

"Maybe I oughtta use The Swede as a potential-meter for all my dates," Bruce countered.

We all shook our heads in agreement at this thought when the inevitable reared its ugly head. Except, as per usual, the head wasn't ugly at all.

"You guys seem to be having a pretty good time," purred the blonde venus who had taken up camp at my buddy Bruce's elbow. A series of exchanged glances spoke volumes.

"Five bucks says the blonde's dust by eleven," cracked The Swede. A five-spot already finding its way out of his pocket and onto the table.

"No dice," says I, "I detect sterner stuff in Bruce's date. The blonde's history by ten thirty." I promptly matched his fiver.

The blonde seemed to take no mind to our pari-mutuel betting at her expense, which indicated to me my money was safe. Approximately three minutes later, or in the time it took the blonde to offer up at least four token chortles at Bruce's tasteless jokes, his date returned. The tension hung in the air like plucked chickens in a delicatessen window. Bruce's date drew first initiative.

"Who's your friend?" she posed to a bemused Bruce. Bemusement is always a risky expression in this type of situation, but by this time Bruce was feeling a bit saucy and decided to throw the dice.

"Ah, (cough, squirm, stall), Linda, let me introduce you to. . .uh, I'm sorry I didn't catch your name."

"Hi!" beamed the blonde. "My name's Cindy, but everybody calls me Bambi. That's my stage name." (giggle)

Bambi? Stage name?

"I'm doubling my bet!" I bellowed. But The Swede would have none of that. As soon as he heard the words "*stage name*" he knew nothing short of a kevlar vest could save the blonde from the barrage she was about to endure.

Bruce's date opened fire. "Listen bimbette. . ."

For the next few moments Linda let loose with a monologue that could only be described as colorful. The number of epithets and rejoiners she tossed out would have made a drunken navy man proud. It was about the time she started in on the blonde's questionable heritage that I cleaned the table of the wagers and stuffed the payout into my emaciated wallet.

The blonde vanished in a flurry of peroxide. For the record, it was precisely ten twenty three and twenty seven seconds, Pacific Standard Time. Needless to say, in our eyes, Linda's stock immediately skyrocketed, split and netted her shareholders a tidy sum. In other words, we were impressed as hell.

To Bambi's credit, what she tried was bold. Tasteless and underhanded, but bold. Of course, a guy would never try something that crass. . .and admit to it.

6
Saving Friends from Themselves

It's a situation we've all been in before. You're out with the buds, the beer goggles are being administered, and your pal's targeting system has just fired. One minute the two of you are making cheap cracks about another buddy's ancestry, the next minute your bud's spotted a babe and is gone in a denim blur. You wave it off, fully expecting him to return, crest-fallen, perhaps still wiping off the beer that's been unceremoniously tossed in his face. But every now and then. . .score!

Nothing can liven up an evening like stumbling upon a "*sure thing:*" that wonderful situation where you don't have to make any effort to get some action, the action comes looking for you. Guys appreciate "*sure things*" much more than women do because women are offered "*sure things*" on a nightly basis; it's not new, exciting or challenging. Guys, on the other hand, could care less. When you're offered the full meal deal at no charge you don't say, "*I'm not hungry.*" Besides, "*sure things*" aren't women with whom you get into two-year relationships. "*Sure things*" are women with whom you get into two-hour relationships. They aren't "*Miss Right,*" they're "*Miss Right Now!*" "*Sure things*" can also be referred to as "*dirty girls,*" but we'll get to that in a later chapter.

Let's go over "*sure thing*" etiquette. It's quite simple: If your buddy's got a "*sure thing*" on the line, and she's pretty good looking, you let him run with it. It she's heinous, you save him. During your efforts to save him, he'll probably put up a fight, but he'll thank you the next day.

Women usually don't understand the concept behind letting your friends go after a "*sure thing.*" They say stuff like, "*Why would you go after someone that drunk? She's obviously a slut. You think that's attractive?*" Etc, etc.

Let me provide you with a humble example.

One time at a community wine-tasting festival, otherwise known as a corporate-sponsored drunk-fest, I got to watch one of my buddies on the prowl. It was a classic situation. These drunk-fests are always high entertainment, because all you have to do is take equal parts men, women and booze, mix vigorously, sit back and watch the fun. An anthropologist with half a brain can see that the line between people and animals becomes increasingly blurred at these events. He could probably base his thesis on animal/human relativity after watching people interact following their seventh glass of wine, and no one would argue his findings.

Felix Unger from The Odd Couple once said there are only two things that separate humans from animals: animals don't use cutlery and humans can control their sexual urges. After the drunk-fest not only would I not trust anyone there with cutlery but I seriously doubt anyone there could *spell* sexual urges, let alone control them.

Let's get back to the subject of our study. My buddy, Dweeb Thingus, is normally a shy, laid-back guy. That changed at the drunk-fest. He had absolutely no problem putting the fin on and cruising the waters in search of prey. Back and forth he patrolled, just below the surface, the fin barely breaking the water. Suddenly, POW! Two women had just left one of the wine booths and Dweeb stepped right up and tossed out the bait.

"Whatcha drinkin?" he offered smartly.

"Wine," came their surprisingly articulate response.

Once the rest of us saw that he was making an effort, we got scarce. Ten minutes later we found him empty-handed and figured they'd simply spit out the hook. Who were we kidding? The day was young, and there was still much wine to drink.

You know how in a car that sucks gas, the higher the RPM needle revs to the right, the quicker the gas needle dips to the left? It's the same thing with booze and inhibitions. The more booze you drink, the less inhibitions you have. It's this concept that makes your twenties such an exciting and hazardous chapter in your life.

Later that day, or should I say about five glasses later, Dweeb stumbled across the women he'd made a play for earlier. And just as he'd hoped, they recognized his now familiar face, were legally drunk and promptly bulldozed their way through the crowd to greet him. The way the one woman was hanging on him it was hard to tell where he stopped and she started. It was at this point that she was affixed the label of "*sure thing.*" It was now only a matter of time before the deed was done.

A woman whom we were there with rolled her eyes and *tsk, tsked* the whole scenario. This promptly got the other guys in the group to roll their eyes at *her* reaction. She didn't get it! She threw out the token comments like, "*Do guys really find that attractive?*" forcing us to defend our buddy.

Let me explain. As I'd alluded to earlier, "*sure things*" don't happen along nearly as much as we'd like. So when they do it's a pleasant surprise--ranking right up there with finding five dollars in the jeans you just pulled out of the dryer, or winning the company super bowl pool on a missed chip-shot field goal. If the "*sure thing*" is very pretty with a great bod, bonus! Ugly "sure things" happen along much more frequently and thus provide the punch line to the old joke *of "Why do guys get drunk?"* The punch line being. . . "*So ugly women can have sex too.*" This doesn't speak too highly of guys, but it's a moral deficiency we've come to accept.

Just as we were getting ready to leave, minus Dweeb of course, I noticed a couple of girls over by one of the wine booths who seemed to be taking an interest in me and my buddies. They were staring, whispering and laughing up a storm. I decided to pull out the old Johnston charm and see if a "*sure thing*" was in my future.

"Hello, ladies. You seem to be having a good time. What was so funny?"

They looked to one another and then burst out laughing again. I took this as a good sign. The brunette with the chardonay finally caught her breath long enough to explain.

"Looking at you and your friends reminded us of a great joke!"

"Do tell? Let's hear it!" I was in like Flynn. Score!

The brunette took another long sip off her wine. "Why do women get drunk. . ?"

7
Beer Goggles

One time, while making chit-chat with a female friend of mine, I commented on a particular night of revelry where I nearly got myself into a rather nasty situation, courtesy of beer goggles. Instead of the warm chuckle of recognition that's normally heard at this time, she floored me with the unthinkable: "What are beer goggles?"

By the time she'd helped me back to my feet and settled me into a booth, my head had begun to clear. Never heard of beer goggles? That's outrageous! I knew public service was in order.

"Ever been out drinking with your pals?"

"Sure," she replied.

"Ever noticed how a guy whom you wouldn't normally give the time of day to suddenly takes on Prince Charming-like qualities after your fifth pint?"

"Sure."

"Beer goggles," said I. It's a common affliction to which only those of the highest moral ground are immune. Beer goggle affliction is usually a precurser to such disturbing maladies as next-morning regret, or late-night humiliation.

Joe Namath once said, at least I think it was Broadway Joe, "*It's two o'clock in the morning. Miss America ain't showing up.*" This perfectly sums up the whole attitude of beer goggles. You know you're hammered. You know your judgment is impaired beyond repair. You know the wildebeast in front of you isn't nearly up to your normally inscrutable standards. . .and yet, you just don't care! By this time the *little head* has devised a bulletproof, iron-clad argument that your alcohol-fogged *big head* cannot refute. All systems are go! It's usually not until one of your more clear-headed buddies saves your bacon or you wake up next to something that looks vaguely similar to a woman you met last night that it occurs to you that this was not a good idea; only you could have sworn the girl you met last night wasn't the spitting image of Bruenhilda, pride of the Bulgarian weigh-lifting team.

Imagine what would happen if someone was resourceful enough to bring a miniature camcorder to the bar, and taped you while you had the beer goggles on. Can you say. . .*extortion*? I think it's safe to say that any aspirations you may have had for a political career would be floating alongside the Charmin.

So, what are the early warning signs that those pesky, reality-distorting goggles are forming? Here are a few red flags to look for: when you're out for chinese food, and you've just spent twenty minutes talking up the restaurant buddah, and then actually came away with a phone number, it's a safe bet the beer goggles have been applied. Or in this case, the saki goggles. (Okay, so saki is Japanese. So sue me.)

When you begin counting off the virtues of the trollop sitting at the bar with sentences like. . ."Those lips, that nose, *that eye!*" It's time to go home.

When your friends notice that the "*girl of your dreams,*" has become "*gorilla your dreams,*" ask the bartender to call a cab.

Everyone has his own way of describing beer-goggles. One analogy would be the time honored "a *two at ten becomes a ten at two.*" And who can argue with "a *four and a six-pack makes a ten?*"

Confused? Let me clarify.

Most individuals of the human race have at one time or another rated others of the same species. You know, "*Great legs! She's definitely an eight.*" Or, "*Check out the loser by the jukebox, he dreams of being a five.*" It's nothing to be terribly proud of, but what the heck. Thus, the two at ten becomes a ten at two refers to said individual being rated, and the time of the rating. Although I'd be hard pressed to drink enough in a four-hour stretch for a lowly two to climb to an almost unreachable ten. But for the good of all mankind I decided to do some hands-on research to determine if it truly is possible.

Me and my two buddies, Dweeb and The Swede, made out for "*Pudgey's House of Hooch*" to carry out the experiment. Being that I was running the experiment and The Swede was our control unit it was up to Dweeb to play the part of the guinea pig.

"So, what do I gotta do?" Dweeb asked.

"Drink excessively and stare at women," I said.

Dweeb considered that for somewhere in the neighborhood of .00008 seconds. "Ok."

"Ok, Dweeb, look at that woman in the corner."

"The one who looks like Sister Griswold from my catholic elementary school?" Dweeb asked with a decidedly pinched expression.

"That would be the one. What do you think? It's now precisely 10 p.m., is she a two?"

"On a good day," Dweeb confessed.

"Excellent. Then let us proceed with the experiment. Drink this beer."

Little did any of the gathered revelers know they were witnessing a first-hand study of the most exacting nature. After approximately two hours I checked my notes and had determined that Dweeb had consumed three beers, a shot of Jack and a surprisingly aggressive little concoction the bartender affectionately called "*The Crippler.*" I made sure to take detailed notes on how he handled the lead-lined tumbler with the ice tongs to keep a safe distance. I'd no idea they kept a welding mask behind the bar.

"Hey, Swede, did you concur with Dweeb's original assessment of the woman in the corner?"

"Yep. I prefer women I have a fighting chance with in an arm-wrestling match."

Fine. All was in order. Our controller had lain the groundwork for the comparison study. It was now midnight, time to check progress.

"Yo, Dweeb. How you feeling?"

"Peachy." slurred Dweeb, except it came out more like "peeshy."

I felt it was time to stoke the fire a bit. "Hey, Dweeb, I think that chick in the corner's giving you the eye." I then gave him a sharp nudge in the ribs.

"Wish one?" garbled Dweeb. It was apparent Dweeb had abandoned all use of sharp consonants. His words had taken on sort of a soft, squishy sound: like his teeth were made of miniature marshmallows and his tongue was jello.

"Her," I prompted, "the one with the olive drab polyester jumpsuit and four inch earrings that look like something my dad insisted on hanging on our christmas tree."

"R'lly? She's givn me th eye?"

"Absolutely." It occurred to me that Dweeb didn't recognize her from earlier on, and the glint that managed to cut though his alcohol-induced cataracts led me to believe she now rated a five in Dweeb's fuzzy brain. She was now worthy of consideration.

"Hey, bartenner!" Dweeb barked with unbridled enthusiasm. "Break out th tongs an mask. I wannanother of those tasty bevergs yu made me."

Moments later he choked down another Crippler and was doing his best to make eye contact with the proposed target. After Dweeb came to the realization that he was unable to hypnotize her from this distance he made his play.

At two in the morning, The Swede and I conferred over our notes and decided to see what kind of dividends our experiment paid out.

It wasn't a pretty sight. Dweeb and target-X were engaged in what at first appeared to be position number twenty seven from the Kama Sutra handbook on middle eastern sexual techniques--and on a barstool for that matter. After marvelling at their astounding balance we proceeded forward.

"Yo, Dweeb. It's showtime. Let's go."

Dweeb broke away while target-X cast us a disproportionately sour glare. "You guys take offff wthout me. I got me a liddle sugr t'nite."

"Oh yeah, Dweeb. She's a looker all right." I then set the bait. "She's an eight if ever I saw one."

"Eight!" scoffed Dweeb, "Shees nuthn short uv a nine! You think I'd waste my time withhh a meeeasly eight?" Dweeb was now caught up in brazen self-rightous indignation, which is no small task after two Cripplers and an assortment of other alcoholic beverages.

What did we managed to glean from this exercise? Our research, which university think-tanks normally would spend thousands of tax-payer dollars on, and which we pulled off for the cost of a few drinks, revealed, beyond a shadow of a doubt, that a two at ten does not actually become a ten at two, but with the correct application of beer goggles is quite capable of becoming a nine. But since "*a two at ten becomes a nine at two*" doesn't make for a snappy-sounding turn-of-phrase we decided not to file our test findings.

8
Pride and Stupidity Cometh Before a Fall

Guys aren't afraid to hurt themselves in the search of a good time. In fact it's encouraged. The best times I've ever recalled usually ended in a fair amount of pain and suffering. It's the guy way. If a guy hasn't spent at least five percent of his life on crutches, with stitches, or recovering from some other self-imposed injury I'm not sure how much I can trust him. A few jammed fingers goes a long way in sizing up another guy. Compound fractures or time in traction is an almost certain bonding element. For guys, the beauty of injuries is the opportunity to regale someone with the story of how they came about.

Women have never really caught on to this practice of sharing injuries with one another. I guess they'll never know the deep respect and admiration one can enjoy from a brief synopsis of the time you went over your handlebars into the electrified barbed-wire fence.

When two guys are enjoying a good laugh over that incident with the M-80 and box of fertilizer. (Who knew fertilizer was highly combustible?) it's just another of the many situations where women get to use their inalienable right to roll their eyes and shake their heads.

There are, of course, some war wounds you're not terribly proud of and only speak of in hushed tones behind closed doors. So please read these next few paragraphs in hushed tones behind a closed door.

I'm ashamed to say, that I'm probably the only person in the history of mankind to break a bone with a nerf ball. You laugh! Hmm, actually so did all my buddies when they saw it happen, so there must be some kind of element of humor to it. Although I was hard-pressed to find it with my hand in a splint for two weeks. If you must know, I broke it playing football. The usual gang was out on a brisk, rainy afternoon in a sufficiently muddy back-lot. About a half hour into the carnage, all two hundred pounds of Spanky Peznick winds up and lets fly with a rocket, right at me. That would have been all well and good except I was only ten feet away. If you've ever played with a wet Nerf football you know they have a tendency to take on an additional ten to fifteen pounds. So basically what I was trying to catch from ten feet away was a speeding shot put. My thirteen year old pinky snapped like a twig and I proceeded to go into my injury ritual that's been known to resemble the Fiji island fire dance.

Crafty toys those nerfs. Deceptive as hell. They should put a warning label on them. "_CAUTION: There is a one in a million chance this product could cause irreparable damage if used in a reckless manner by a complete moron._" If I had seen such a label I would have doubtlessly been more cautious.

Another embarrassing injury I had was the age-old favorite "_whack upside the head._" Everyone knows that if you ever get a black eye or some other impossible-to-hide facial wound the standard excuse is that you walked into a door--always has, always will. Although I always wondered what could sound more stupid than walking into a door. At any rate, one time in a hotel room I had the distinct displeasure of living out that favorite excuse: I actually walked into a door; opened my forehead up like a cheap can of tuna.

When the hotel doctor showed up he found me lying comfortably on the bed with an icepack on my face. Upon lifting the ice pack he screamed and placed the pack back over my face, which struck me not only as reasonably unprofessional but rather disconcerting as well.

"Good God, man! What happened to your face?"

"Nothing happened to my face. It's just a cut."

After I assured the doctor that, other than the one wound, that's what I normally look like, I settled him down enough to take a closer peek at my forehead.

"So how'd you get this divot in your noggin'?" he asked, still scanning my face with a look that seemed to say, "_I've got a brother-in-law who's a crack plastic surgeon._"

"I walked into a door."

"Uh-huh. Sure you did."

"No, really. I did walk into a door."

"Yeah. Of course you did."

At this point I sat up with slightly more than a trace of annoyance. "You don't believe me, do you? I did! I did! I did walk into a door!"

The doctor had slowly eased his way over to the phone and was quickly punching numbers as he kept a wary eye on me and, with his most soothing voice, kept repeating, "Of course you did, of course you did."

At this point I began screaming and jumping up and down with frustration. "I did, I did, I did, I did too walk into a door!"

I think the jumping up and down was a bad idea.

Seconds later the door burst in and two orderlies, who I could have sworn were featured on "America's Most Wanted," rushed in and pinned me to the bed. The doctor had shaken off his soothing bed-side manner and began shouting and waving about. "I'll need fifty cc's of thorazine and restraints! We may have a psychotic patient with brain damage!"

It took me three hours and twelve phone calls before I could get one of my friends to vouch for my character and convince the medical staff that, if it really was me in their care, that I probably did walk into a door. I must admit I felt a little bad for the doctors. They were pretty excited, thinking they'd stumbled upon some new form of psychosis and couldn't wait for the grant money to come pouring in.

The crease in my head is certainly not a scar I take pride in. But it's nothing compared to the injury incurred by Nob, "*the human party favor*." For the sake of simplicity we'll just call it "*the eyelid incident*."

It started out innocuously enough. The nasty injuries usually do. Several of us had been hanging out in classic guy fashion; draped over chairs and couches watching Daffy Duck cartoons. Little did Nob know that within minutes he'd be caught in the middle of an act of fate no one could have ever imagined. The irony of the whole thing was that here was Nob howling with glee over Daffy's tragic injuries, and five minutes later it would be us howling with glee over Nob's.

After the final cartoon ran its course and Daffy had gotten his bill blown off for the twelfth time, we flipped off the tube and made our farewells. It was a reasonably cold day out and all of us had brought coats along. Nob had one of those fleece liners that only zips down about halfway, just enough to get your head through. But when Nob slipped the coat over his head, his arms still above him as he tried to push them into the sleeves, he stopped.

"Ow. What the hell?"

We all turned to look at Nob, standing there with his coat halfway over his head, his arms standing straight up like goal posts.

"What's up, Nob?"

Nob began reaching down to his hidden face, his hands still only three quarters of the way up the sleeves.

"Ow. Ow. Ow!"

"Nob, what are you doing?" I asked as the rest of the gang got a good chuckle at this strange sight.

"I can't get my coat on. The zipper's caught on my eyelid."

We all glanced around at each other with incredulous looks. "Nob, did you just say you've zipped your eyelid?"

"Yes, I've zipped my stupid eyelid. Now help me get it off!"

Nob began to squirm and shift around, trying to reach down to his face with his tentacle-like sleeves.

This was too good to be true! At first we tried to keep straight faces and be concerned for Nob's welfare but quickly abandonned that idea for huge gales of laughter instead.

"Har-har-har!"

Upon hearing our outburst Nob fought even more feverishly with the coat, which now took on the appearance of some great purple alien that was attempting to swallow his upper torso. It seemed the alien was succeeding.

"This isn't funny guys! Ow! Ow! Ow!!! This hurts like a son-of-a-bitch!"

"Har-har-har!" we continued bellowing.

I've come to the conclusion that the best laughs are at other people's expense. I don't remember finding too much humor in the time my buddy Dweeb stuck a stick in my spoke, sending me flying over the handlebars into the stickerbushes, but seeing Nob hop around, ranting and cursing in pain, struck me as just about the funniest thing I could ever imagine. If he had been hopping around, ranting and cursing just for fun, it wouldn't have been half as hilarious. But knowing he was in pain because his eyelid was caught in the zipper was just too much for my humor sensors to process. I doubled up into a ball on the floor and went into laughing convulsions. There wasn't too much floor space left because my other pals had already taken up residence there.

The louder Nob's cries of anguish and fury got, the harder we laughed.

"Har-har-har-har-har-har. . ."

For a moment I thought I might cause myself some horrible injury through this uncontrollable laughter, and it would be me who would be the target of my friend's sniggering. I was helpless! All I could do was lie there shaking, letting out little squeaks that, had my stomach muscles not knotted up, would probably have been deep belly laughs. In fact, none of the guys were getting out very good chuckles either. They'd all been reduced to those short barks and wheezes that come out when you've laughed yourself beyond the point of human endurance. If anyone had been drinking milk at the time, it would have been surely streaming out his nostrils, ears and both eyeballs too!

We finally started settling down after a few well-placed kicks by Nob.

By the time we'd manage to get back on our feet again, it only took one more look at Nob standing there with the coat over his head and his arms above his head to send us reeling again.

"Har-har-har-har!"

Nob again shuffled around the room, administering kicks to groins and breadbaskets to return us to some semblace of order.

Here we are with just another classic difference between men and women. While most women may have laughed, oh-so-briefly, at their poor friend's plight, they would have been immediately hit with an annoying wave of sympathy and begin administering soothing words of comfort. The only words of comfort you'd hear guys give to their stricken friend at this time would be, *"What kind of dumb ass zips up his eyelid?"* or maybe, *"You have no idea how stupid you look right now! I'll bet that hurts like hell! Har-har-har*!" Sympathy never has been one of our strong points.

It was now apparent that Nob couldn't get the zipper off his eyelid without taking the eyelid with it, so we herded him into the car and drove to the emergency room. It was a good thing Nob couldn't see, what with the coat still over his head, because he would have gotten even more pissed after seeing us gritting our teeth in an effort not to bust a gut again. We drove on in silence, holding in our laughter, using an iron will none of us realized we had. We then drew straws to see who would be the lucky one who got to tell the emergency room receptionist what we had for them. I wasn't about to leave this opportunity to chance so I cheated.

"Wait right here, Nob. I'll get an orderly."

Thirty seconds later a huge storm of laughter erupted from the emergency room reception area. Nob just sat in the back seat with his tentacles above his head.

You'll be glad to know that after three hours of surgery and numerous wisecracks from the head surgeon, Nob got to keep his eyelid. They did have to cut his coat up though, but Nob didn't care. He was thrilled to be able to trade the tentacles in for arms again.

Apart from the really embarrassing injuries, the urge to do physical damage to oneself is a desire instilled in men at an early age. Let me give you a humble example.

I was eight years old; definitely old enough to know better but stupid enough not to care.

On maps the slope was designated 47th avenue, but to any kid on the block it was, "*Dead-man's hill*" or, "*The Widow-Maker*." No boys who grew up in the neighborhood reached adolescence without knowing the terrible wrath of "*The Widow-Maker*." Of course, being boys, just reaching adolescence was an impressive stunt in itself.

There was something magical about the hill; alluring. You couldn't go near it without an overwhelming desire to race to the top and test the theories of gravity, terminal velocity and your parent's medical plan. Speeding down the hill in the contraption of your choice was sort of a local initiation. A "*baptism by fire*" or, "*by pavement,*" as it were. By my eighth birthday I began feeling the primordial urges. It was time for my journey into manhood.

But the vehicle? I had witnessed an assortment over the years-from skateboards to bicycles to go-carts. Since the bicycle method was strictly for whimps and wannabes, I scanned my memory for the last time someone made the attempt on a skateboard. It was a lad named Bark Whipple, may he rest in peace. If memory serves, it wasn't pretty. I've got to hand it to him though, he was making outstanding time until his wheels locked up when he hit the gravel. No one has yet to break the distance record he set from where he lifted off the skateboard to where he landed in the rhododendron bushes. After recalling the ensuing ruckus, what with the police cars and ambulances, I made a quick decision in favor of the go-cart method.

There were, of course, extenuating circumstances in my decision to risk life and limb for the sake of impressing my buddies. As is frequently the case when guys do something stupid; a woman was involved.

Her name was Dawn Miller; a fine figure of a woman at nine (an older woman, she, six months my senior). She lived across the street, and, on more than one occasion, I found myself picking pebbles out of my skinned knees after aborted attempts to impress her with my acrobatic prowess on a Schwinn one-speed.

Dawn didn't usually give me the time of day but if anything would turn her head it would be a run down *"Dead-man's hill."* I caught her out on her front lawn playing with her Barbies and rolled by to casually drop the bomb on her.

"Hey, Dawn. Whatcha doin'?"

"Playing." (Women: masters of the one-word reply.)

"Didja hear someone's gonna take on *'The Widow-Maker'* on Saturday?"

"Nope." So far she had managed to not give me even the slightest glance, damn her, so I felt I'd better haul out the heavy artillery.

"Guess who's doin it?" I remarked as casually as I could.

"Who." It was a statement, not a question. Posed, I'm sure, to infuriate me further. I opened the bomb doors and let her fly.

"Me."

The reaction was instantaneous and highly rewarding.

"You? You're gonna take on *'The Widow-Maker?'* Are you crazy? Wow! Can I watch? I've never seen a real ambulance up-close before!" Her unbridled enthusiasm filled me with euphoria- the type of euphoria that usually leads to doing something incredibly stupid.

I told her what time the great event would take place and decided to leave it at that. I rode away, feeling her new-found respect wash over me like water from a sprinkler on an August afternoon.

With my newly bolstered confidence I prepared for the next phase in my conquest of *"The Widow-Maker;"* building the craft! A brief search of the neighborhood garbage cans and dump sites resulted in the appropriate equipment. A carelessly discarded apple box, some baling wire, and a partially dismantled Radio-Flyer wagon made a secure if somewhat drafty framework. A hubcap from a '68 Plymouth Valiant made for an excellent steering mechanism and two milk jugs filled with sand and tied to the chassis would surely bring the vehicle to a complete stop when thrown out the back. I was dismayed at what people recklessly threw away. What treasures!

When the fateful day finally arrived, my trusty friend Lefty Gristle helped me drag the go-cart up the hill for its maiden voyage. Standing on the summit I knew then how Celtic kings felt when surveying their domain: Power! Lining the hill were the neighborhood kids. No one missed a run on *"The Widow-Maker;"* a classic example of morbid curiosity.

I lowered myself into the cockpit and looked to Lefty for the countdown.

"Do I get your baseball card collection when you don't make it?" Lefty asked.

I hauled in the milk jugs as I enjoyed Lefty's humor. That was one of the things I liked about Lefty, his ability to look so serious during his best gags.

When the countdown reached one, I pushed off and the go-cart creaked to life. Within seconds I was ambling down the hill at a speed I was sure would break the sound barrier. That was until I saw Lefty jogging along side hollering encouragement. Eventually gravity took its toll and Lefty was left eating my dust.

The rush was incredible--bugs pinging off my face, wheels shrieking as they made sporatic contact with the pavement. Now, I'm not the most handy guy in the world. Building things with precision isn't one of my strong points and it was during this experience that that point was, if you'll pardon the expression, driven home. I was approximately half way down the hill when I noticed that my automotive designs were slightly askew. I began to veer left at an angle best described as acute, sending kids scattering like frightened sparrows. I wrenched the hubcap/steering wheel to the right and was amazed at how far it flew when it came off in my hands. The thought of, "*Why have I been wasting my time with a stupid frisbee all summer?*" managed to slip into my brain, somehow. I'm not sure where it found the space, considering most of my grey matter was preoccupied with survival instincts.

My extreme portside navigation continued, unabated, at a blurring pace. The last thing I remembered was the look of horror on the faces of my neighborhood compatriots as they broke rank and ran for cover. It was a very satisfying last thing to remember.

When I awoke, you can imagine my joy to discover I was in a hospital. I was wrapped up like a mummy and had these cool splint-like things on my arms and legs. This was better than I could have imagined! My buddies were probably hoping I didn't survive the ordeal, knowing full well that if I lived they'd get to hear about it for the next seventy years. I plan on proving their fears correct.

Yep, it was the kind of day most boys dream of. I impressed the hell out of my childhood sweetie, I scared the bejeezus out of most of the kids in the neighborhood and had the scars to back up all my boasts.

Were there any drawbacks to this spectacular event? Well sure, airport metal detectors seem to have a heck of a time with that plate in my head and those steel pins in my arm.

9
The Telephone Obsession

Since communication, or lack there of, seems to be the principal gripe about men, let's take a look at one of the links in the communication chain: the telephone.

Let's cut to the chase. Women like talking on the phone more than men. It's Ma Bell, right? Not Pa Bell. That should tell you something right there. You talk on the phone with your girlfriend and when you've run out of things to talk about you hang up, right? Ha! Fat chance. They want to chat until your tongue looks like a banana that's been sitting in the sun for too long.

This woman/phone anomaly can be traced back to their formative years. Women reach their phone peak at around sixteen, before tailing off a bit as they grow older. Their plateau, however, still hovers miles above men's.

When a man discovers his wife is pregnant, if he has any business acumen whatsoever, he will want to know if it's a boy or a girl immediately. If it's a girl he has to start some sort of financial plan as early as possible. Thirty seconds after the doctor points out the necessary details on the ultra-sound the dad-to-be should already be halfway up the street to his financial advisor. And any broker worth his salt will know enough about "*phone-financing*" to recommend a good portfolio.

"So, Mister Farnsworth, expecting a little one are we?"

"Yep. We peeked. It's a girl."

"Excellent! And congratulations! It's a good thing you came to me now. We should be able to build a fine nest egg for you by the time she reaches her formidable phone years. Now, let's get some facts out in advance so we know what we're building for. Will she have any brothers or sisters?"

"No. We're only planning on one child. Does that matter?"

The broker then begins tapping his bic fine-line and punching a few more keys on the keyboard while perusing the list of stocks, bonds and mutual funds on the computer screen. "I'm afraid it does. No siblings usually results in accelerated phone usage. I'd suggest a strong, aggressive growth, mutual fund."

Most parents save money for their child's college education. The exceptionally bright parents with daughters double the figure to take phone expenses into account. I remember reading in the paper about a man who was busted for trying to knock over a liquor store. He told the police the reason he'd done it was because he'd gotten his little girl a separate phone line. The poor sap had no idea what he was getting into. It was break-and-enter or sell his sports car. At least it was an easy decision.

When I was younger I'd heard about the mysterious woman/phone thing but never gave it much consideration, at least not until I met it face to face.

I was fifteen, still wet behind the ears and only slightly less knowledgable about the dealings of women than I am now. In other words, my knowledge was comparable to an ant's fart in the grand canyon.

I'd met a sweet young thing at the skating rink and that night gave her a call. For the first half hour we covered the typical mundane stuff that fifteen years olds find riveting: school stuff, movie stuff, friends of friends stuff—the usual. I happily babbled on, feeling quite proud at my ability to hold up my end of the conversation. But by the sixtieth minute she began to show her stamina, where I could see mine ebbing like the tide. She pounded on at a staggering pace, peppering me with a flurry of questions. It was all I could do to keep from hitting the canvas. I made a desperate attempt at curtailing the conversation but, like the true veteran she was, she deftly side-stepped my puny efforts and drove headlong into another assault on my eardrum.

By the ninety-minute mark I was holding onto the ropes, oblivious to her assault. I numbly blurted out answers of "yeah," "sure," "I'll bet," and probably countless others I couldn't recall later. She pressed on with all the singlemindedness of a starving pit bull.

I must admit, I was astonished at her vocal endurance and her admirable ability to carry on a conversation with someone who had become as talkative as a cigar store indian. In fact, I think she even got stronger in the later rounds. Mercifully, after two hours her father had found the proper power tools to break into her room and get her off the phone. I crumpled in a heap at the foot of my bed, wasted and withered like a pile of dry leaves. My tongue had swollen to the size of a prize-winning kumquat and my larynx felt like it had just finished a forced march through the Mojave desert.

I tried to yell to my mom for help but all that came out was sort of a pathetic honk. The honk didn't roust my mother but seemed to make a strong enough impression on some migrating geese that were passing over the house that my dad had to fight them off with a rake.

The next day, the school nurse, after sticking a tongue depressor far enough down my esophagus that I could have sworn I felt it in my lower intestine, shook her head and smiled knowingly. "Are we seeing a new girl these days?"

"How'd you know?" I honked, quickly ducking in case another flock of geese was somewhere within earshot.

"Typical symptoms. Did we call her on the phone last night?"

I was dumbfounded. Her insight rivaled the amazing Kreskin! One look down my throat and she had somehow managed to zero-in on the workings of my social life. I sat there with a slightly more stupefied look on my face than normal. "As a matter of fact I did call her last night," I honked again.

"I'd suggest limiting your phone conversations to thirty-minutes from now on or you might want to consider renting yourself out to hunters as a goose-caller."

Her wisdom was well beyond her years. It wasn't until I was much older that I learned all men get their vocal chords pummeled through reckless phone practices. Luckily it's something we learn at an early age so we can develop our own ploys of getting out of extended phone conversations.

I wonder if women had such hyper-strong voice boxes before the advent of the telephone? No doubt, over the years their bodies have adapted to this symbiotic bond between themselves and the telephone.

With technology speeding forward at such an alarming rate, one can't help but wonder what other inventions will alter women's physiology. Will they all just keep pushing the physical boundaries until they've become a race of uber-babes?

Alexander Graham Bell, what hath thou wrought?

10
The Translator

I have a friend. His name is Nob; and Nob has a translator built into his head. I have no idea how it got there, or in which part of the brain it is, but I know it's there. I've seen it in action. If I were a betting man, and I am, I'd wager you too have a friend like Nob--a friend with a translator. You just didn't know that's what it was. You probably just thought your friend was sort of dweebish, a social misfit, or had a hearing impediment. You had no idea he had this evil device wired into his skull.

Let me elaborate on the translator and how it works. The only way I became privy to this fascinating discovery was through constant exposure to Nob. The repetition factor of Nob's strange behaviour became so high it could no longer be ignored. After about the ninety-fourth time Nob did something really odd I began trying to predict what would happen in given situations. After successfully predicting his bizarre actions over and over I knew something was up. His methods were not those of a normal human being and, thus, I concluded there were other forces at work; forces obviously beyond Nob's control. I mean, what other explanation could there be? People don't act that weird, that often, by choice.

Let me explain. If, for example, a woman was talking to Nob and she said, "*Hi, Nob, I'm Lisa. Nice meeting you. Maybe I'll see you around sometime.*" To the average person what she said is precisely what they would hear. But not so with Nob. What Nob would hear would be roughly translated to, "*Hi, Nob, I'm Lisa. I want to have sex with you.*"

Notice anything peculiar? Let's go back and look at the original sentence and compare it to what Nob hears.

"*Hi, Nob. I'm Lisa.*" Ok, fine. Nothing lost in translation here. But now let's go to the meat of the sentence. How does, "*Nice meeting you. Maybe I'll see you around sometime,*" magically become, "*I want to have sex with you.*"? They're not even phonetically similar! I'm sure right now some of you are thinking, "*Hey, my buddy Nick's done that before, too!*" Sadly, your buddy Nick probably has a translator as well.

There is one advantage to having a friend with a translator, however. You can always count on him doing something with high entertainment value. Friends with translators should always be invited to parties, because it's a safe bet they're going to entertain more people than they piss off. And the entertainment value has residual effects as well. Whenever someone with a translator does something completely out of left field it's guaranteed to be discussed over beers on countless nights. That's why people with translators are also known as "human party favors."

Nob is the best human party favor I know. He's always guaranteed to do something bizarre. He only pisses off three or four people at the party, depending on how much success he's having swooping on women, and his stories have become the stuff of numerous side-splitting recollections. Let me entertain you with one such incident.

The evening involved a festive gathering. The parents cruised out of town and the friends immediately cruised into the house. . .beverages in hand, or hands if they're real friends.

It was early August, and time for the semi-annual "We're-having-a-party-for-no-reason-other-than-the-fact-that-Mom-and-Dad-are-out-of-town" party. The day involved steaks on the barbie and schmoozin' with the gang. I, of course, had my girlfriend in attendance, and that made my friends happy. In an earlier chapter I noted that if a guy brings a good-looking girl with him it kind of pisses off his buddies because they know they can't hit on her. But if she's an established girlfriend it's OK cuz she's just part of the gang. In this situation she was an established girlfriend so there were no feelings of animosity. In fact, since she was part of the gang, *and* a babe, the guys were excited she was there. Not only could they ogle her and get away with it because they're friends, they knew she'd bring her babe friends too. It's a simple fact that good-looking women travel in packs.

Nob, "*the human party favor*," wasn't the only guy swoopin' on my girlfriend's pals, and he certainly wasn't the only one chugging a few cold ones. But he was the one who was the recipient of the following morning wisecracks.

What can I say? He deserved every dig.

At different times during the evening I saw Nob jabbering away with this gal named Lisa. I didn't pay much attention to what they were talking about, I just figured it for idle chitchat. Of course, idle chitchat when the translator is working can be a recipe for disaster.

Later in the evening, however, a flustered Nob came stumbling up to me to ask what Lisa's problem was. He'd been talking to her for a full half hour and not once did she say, "*Nob, I want to have sex with you. Take me away. I'm a dirty girl.*"

We figured that since Lisa was much older than the women Nob was used to swooping on, easily twenty-two, Nob must have had expectations of nothing less than full body contact by now. When he wasn't getting the proper rapport he vented his frustration toward me.

"Oh yeah. Real cool," he blustered angrily. "She's strictly minor-league material. I thought she was ready for The Show but no chance. She's nothing but single-A ball!" (See chapter on speaking in sports metaphors.)

That, of course, didn't mean Nob was going to give up. He was quite sure that as more drinks went down the hatch, she still might get the call to the big league club.

Sure enough, some time during the evening, Nob's translator kicked in. As the night was winding down Nob made yet another attempt at Lisa. Little did she know that the words coming out of her mouth were not the words entering Nob's ears. She made the often fatal mistake of ending the conversation with the wrong words. She said, "*See you later.*"

Wrong, wrong, wrong.

You see, Nob hears that and thinks, "*Cool! She's finally stepping to the plate. She's going to bed soon. She wants to see me. . .in bed! Later. Yes. Score!*"

The party had pretty much run its course, so after checking to make sure all the passed-out bodies were still breathing, I went to bed.

I was lying there, looking directly out the door toward the hallway, and there I saw Nob; smiling triumphantly, licking his chops, and giving me the thumbs up sign! He then leaned forward and opened the door to the neighboring bedroom.

"*Odd,*" I thought, "*Lisa was crashed in that bedroom. I don't remember Nob and Lisa hitting it off that well.*"

Apparently Nob wasted little time peeling his gear and hopping into the sack. I calculate that it took Lisa somewhere around six seconds to evaluate the situation and beat a hasty retreat. A dazed and confused Lisa walked out of the room and into the hallway. She looked over at me, shook her head in disbelief, and continued out of sight to find refuge on one of the unoccupied couches.

I didn't see Nob reappear until the following morning, at which point my friends and I unceremoniously grilled him on his late-night rendezvous with Lisa.

"Weird," He said rather disgruntedly, "I don't know what her problem is. She told me she wanted to hook up with me later. When I got into bed and started grabbin', she got up and left! Go figure. I thought she was ready for the bigs, but she ain't nothing but minor league."

Lisa returned later that morning in search of her stuff. But some of her stuff was missing; her shoes were gone.

After a frustrating search we found the shoes lying under a shrub in the backyard.

Apparently, after being denied access, Nob decided to get even. So he did what any mature, thirty-year-old gentleman would do. . .he pitched her shoes out the second-story window.

Let this be a lesson to you all. The next time you show up at a party it's always wise to check with the host to see if anyone there has a translator. A good host will get this information in advance to warn any potential victims. And, if you see someone you'd like to meet at the party, don't be afraid to ask around if that tall, dark stranger with whom you've locked eyes has been known to misinterpret conversations.

It might just save you a barefoot walk home.

11
Blind Dates

To most people the term "*blind date*," has equal connotation to terms such as "*root canal*," *or "compound fracture.*" Why is this so? This impulsive distrust obviously stems from our basic fear of the unknown. I, for one, have never had the same knee-jerk response to blind dates as most people. You see, my parents met on a blind date so I figure if it worked for them, why not me? Probably because their blind date was almost fourty years ago when people still used words like "*swell*," and "*keen*." In today's more sophisticated social dramas blind dates just aren't the same. Although I must admit there are still basic similarities between blind dates fourty years ago and blind dates now, such as, your friends still lie like dogs when describing your date.

Case in point: my "*friend*" Dweeb tells me his sister's husband's dentist's hygienist saw me out with a couple of buds and wanted to know if I was seeing anybody. After successfully dodging my best flinty stare Dweeb thrilled to the chance of telling me how he gladly gave up the sought-after information. Dweeb obviously hadn't quite forgiven me for that incident last summer concerning a video recorder, a very drunken Dweeb and his parole officer's daughter. Like I was supposed to know she was his parole officer's daughter. At any rate, Dweeb begins the dance, and starts greasing me up like a u-joint on a '64 Barracuda.

" 'Oh,' I told her, 'You bet he's single! 'Bout the singlest guy I know.'" Dweeb's enjoying the moment, so I let him run with it.

"'Bertha,' I says. . ." (Dweeb's sister has the unfortunate distinction of being the only woman on the face of God's green Earth to actually have the name "Bertha." But then Dweeb's parents always did have a rather twisted sense of humor considering "Dweeb" isn't a nickname.) "'. . .you tell that young bicuspid babe she couldn't have picked a better guy. Ol' Bryan's one in a million,' says I."

Dweeb continued warming to the role of defender of my good name, and who was I to stop him from pumping a few extra PSI into my ego? Dweeb went on for a good eight minutes on what a stellar slice of manhood I was and that this girl oughtta be thanking her maker that I even consider gracing her with my valuable time. I, of course, knew Dweeb was only regaling me with this praise so I wouldn't cold-cock him for getting me into this situation. Damned if it didn't work, too. I think it was the part about the stellar slice of manhood that clinched it for me.

I told him I'd consider it but first I needed some information. This is the point where all blind dates resemble die-cast molds cut on the same assembly line. Here's where your friend's years of polishing the fine art of lying come to a head. And the parts that aren't bold-faced lies are merely impressive displays of footwork.

"So, what's she look like?" I begin.

"She's a hygienist, you know. Also works nights as the manager at Dairy Queen. And they don't pass out that kind of responsibility to just anyone," Dweeb countered.

"Right. So, what's she look like?" I continued.

"Super dancer! She'll cut a rug like an exacto!" Dweeb dodged.

"Uh-huh. So, what's she look like?"

"I'll bet you can get free dilly bars and discount checkups if you go out with her!" Dweeb offered.

This went on for some time: me advancing with "So, what's she look like?" and Dweeb giving me information my mom would trade government secrets for but is patently useless to me. Finally, after a good six rounds of evasive action he finally gave in.

"All right, all right. If you have to know, I hear she's pretty hot--won some kind of pageant back home. I just didn't want you going out with her for the wrong reasons."

"What kind of pageant? Miss Inbred 1997? I don't want to waste an evening with a woman with more hair on her chest than me."

I eventually caved in and called my mystery date up. She actually sounded very pleasant on the phone, but no way was I going to be suckered by that. How many times in your lifetime have you built up an image in your head of that cool-sounding disc jockey only to be crushed to discover he/she looks remarkably like your elementary school janitor; the one everyone swears lives in a wooden box in the school's basement. And if you had the guts to sneak down there, rumor had it you'd also find the remains of Barney Cotlip after the janitor found him standing on a chair to sneak peeks through the exhaust fan into the girls lavatory. No one really believed the principal's feeble explanation that Barney's family simply moved to Bismarck, North Dakota. No one moves to Bismarck, North Dakota.

I agreed to meet my mystery date, "*Cheryl*," at a pizza place downtown. I made sure I practiced a good sniffle and an occasional sneeze in case I needed to use the old "*not feeling well*" ploy.

Upon entering the restaurant I noticed a gorgeous woman sitting at a table, glancing around, obviously waiting for someone. She looked my way and instantly waved me over. My heart sang! I couldn't believe my luck. Good old Dweeb. Whatta guy! I knew he wouldn't burn me. Who'd have figured a babe like that would need a blind date?

Approximately halfway through my rapture a large, perfectly coiffed man shouldered by me to take up residence with my blind date. It was about that moment that lightning struck and I realized she'd been waving to him, standing behind me. At about the same moment I felt a tap on my shoulder and heard that pleasant-sounding voice from behind.

"You must be my date," she chirped.

Could this be it? Is my future wife standing behind me right now? Will this be "love at first sight?" I turned around and. . . and. . .

Reality caught me with a good stiff uppercut to the chin.

She wasn't really fat. Of course she wasn't really thin either. She was, as my dad would say, "*solid.*" Women usually have some sort of curves to their shape. On this woman, I could detect no such thing. I'm sure that had I a tape measure I could have used the same length of tape for all three measurements. Her hair had a distinctly frail quality to it, with a color I'm not sure exists in nature. Her pale, waxy complexion was highlighted by several unfortunately arranged blemishes that no amount of hydrogen peroxide could conquer. The jack boots she wore looked like they were taken right off the feet of some modern-day storm trooper. And the frock that hung so elegantlessly over her looked like something that would have probably sent any fashion afficionado kneeling before the great white porcelain goddess. I've never really seen a fabric that absorbed all forms of light and color so efficiently. I wondered if NASA knew about it.

Of course, what topped it off were the twelve earrings and the large diamond stud in the side of her nose. Maybe it's just me but if I was born with a big shiny silver wart on my schnoz I'd want it removed. Yet she went out of her way, and paid, to get one put on! I must be getting old.

We sauntered over to a booth and I did my best to lighten the situation with some clever banter.

"A lot of my friends give me a bad time about my plaid coat but I didn't figure you'd mind, considering you're a '*blind*' date. Heh-heh."

No smile. No grin. No smirk. She just looked me over with a bland look of suppressed annoyance.

"You know of course that polyester is a petroleum by-product," she pointed out. "Petroleum like in oil, like in the Exxon Valdez, like in hundreds of thousands of innocent birds and animals dead thanks to consumers who find it necessary to wear synthetic fabrics."

So much for clever banter.

I figured I'd move on to something safer. "Would you like some wine?"

Her look of suppressed annoyance abandonned the suppressed part and went straight to annoyance. "Wine? As in grapes? Picked by migrant workers for slave wages, while forced to live in abject poverty?"

"You're right. Forget the wine. How about a cup of coffee?"

"Coffee? Columbian coffee? From the farms of South American coffee growers acting as fronts for the Columbian drug cartels? Suppliers of our urban city youth? Offering them the only visible means of dragging themselves out of poverty only to bring them crashing down to a world of crime and death? I'll pass."

This wasn't shaping up the way I'd hoped. "Ok, anyone being oppressed by the tea-makers?"

"A nice cup of earl grey would be nice."

Success! Moments later our tea arrived.

"Would you like some sugar with that?" I offered.

"Processed sugar?"

Mercifully our pizza arrived soon after (one half pepperoni, one half goat cheese and artichoke hearts. Guess which side was mine). By the time we'd finished

I'd learned more about Marxist doctrine than I would have preferred. I'll give her one thing, even though she tried desperately to show me the error of my ways, I came out of the conversation feeling remarkably happy with my capitalist lifestyle.

It wasn't long before I picked up on her sniffling and sneezing. Suddenly she glanced at her watch and announced that she wasn't feeling very well. She thanked me for the wonderful evening, let loose with one last artificial sneeze and bolted for the door.

I was shocked. What a transparent ploy! I couldn't believe she could be so shallow! I sat there in stunned silence for, oh, a good three seconds before whistling over to the exit. If I hurried there might still be some good hunting at the "*What's Your Sign?*" nightclub and lounge.

12
Stage Fright at the Urinal

If you wrote up a list of things that one sex has to put up with that the other doesn't, there's no doubt the women's list would be longer. Every guy on the planet has heard a few of these things listed at one time or another.

"*You men have it so easy. You don't have to go through things like childbirth, periods, yeast infections, etc. etc. etc.*"

True. But in all fairness to men, I've decided to even the playing field a little by letting women in on a nasty little annoyance men must tolerate that women don't.

It's called, "*stage fright,*" also known as, "*performance anxiety.*"

No, I'm not talking about theatre, I'm talking about

public bathrooms. You know, those wonderful places where men don't have to wait in line but women can grow moss by the time they get inside. You'd think since women have bladders the size of a peanut and make trips to the restroom approximately seven times more than men, that the architectural geniuses who design buildings would put in seven times as many ladies rooms as men's rooms. But that, sadly, is not the case. But don't worry ladies, you'll be glad to know that even though we can rush in and out in the time it takes hummingbirds to mate, we occasionally meet up with an embarrassing situation known as stage fright. That not-so-golden moment when the brain is willing but the body is unable. When you stand there, at the urinal or trough, with a half-dozen total strangers at your side. . .and wait. But nothing happens.

When you recognize the early phases of stage fright the temperature in your hands drops about twelve degrees. Your sweat-glands begin having the time of their lives while you take a deep breath and try to relax. Seconds magically stretch into hours as you desperately wait for something to happen. Nothing. You begin to stare at the wall in front of you and marvel at the impressive grout work done by a loyal member of Local 185. You glance right and left at your next-door neighbors, proudly streaming forth, chuckle to yourself, and make a feeble comment to no one in particular that sounds something like, "*Heh, guess he doesn't like to perform in front of a crowd. Heh. Heh.*"

Your neighbors cast a sheepish grin in your direction, thanking whatever deities that are handy that it's not them making the feeble excuses.

After making your token chuckle, you flush for no reason other than habit and to drown out the silence surrounding your space. You promptly tuck the noncomplying member back into its home and slink away, vainly trying to keep a grip on what's left of your self-respect.

An interesting medical sidenote to stage fright is that it makes your sense of hearing rival that of our canine friends, when you realize that the most obtrusive sound in the bathroom is the silence from your urinal. Of course if you had any idea you'd be struck dry you would've hidden your shame in a stall, but no man knows when it's his time to be rendered mute at the trough.

Since guys don't exactly discuss this problem at length it's generally difficult to get specifics on why some are afflicted and others are not. Is it the color of the walls, the number of people present, lack of stall doors, dividers between the urinals, the trough, the mirrors? Just what causes this malady? I decided to go to the source and get some answers. I went to my friend Yank Pudweller.

Like others of his kind, Yank doesn't like to talk about it much, but was willing to speak in the interest of science. Yank says there are plenty of others out there just like him. He's seen 'em. They've seen him. They understand each other.

They look no different from you or me, but behind closed doors, it's another world. For those afflicted, entering the sacred room is scary in itself, but an *empty* room can help buffer that fear. Of course an empty bathroom without a door lock is still risky. You're always fearful someone will come in at the moment of truth. No lock. No privacy. No dice.

According to Yank, the key is getting started. Once you're on your way then you're cool. Smooth sailing! If Yank enters an empty restroom and finds no shoes in the neighboring stalls then he'll have the belt, button, zipper and boxers out of the way in milliseconds. He wastes no time, because that door could swing open at any moment.

Yank told me of a bathroom experience where he was just getting ready to release the biological storm-drains when the door popped open. Immediately shaken by the arrival of the untimely intruder, the necessary internal organs decided to take a coffee break. Yank just had to stand there. The new person stepped up next to Yank, and well, he just stood there, too.

There was that eerie silence we discussed earlier, followed by the always popular toe-tapping, and of course the occasional drip. . .drip. The two of them were just looking around the room, painfully uncomfortable. Soon the other guy zipped up, sheepishly muttered, "*I understand*," and walked back to the sink where he started washing his hands. He was giving Yank a little time to be alone. Soon enough, the organs got back to work, the cracks in the dam gave way and Yank was relieved. Yank thanked the man and went his way. The other guy was a "*special*" person too.

Another pal of mine, Schlep Weeblow, has been known to have bouts of stage fright as well. But his affliction has an interesting twist. He only gets stage fright at troughs, not urinals. For Schlep, performing at a trough isn't unlike teeing off on the first hole with a gallery watching. That's always the time you pull out a duck-hook that would send your average mathematician scrambling for his slide-rule and abacus to prove no object can travel in that erratic a manner. In effect, whenever Schlep steps up to a trough, he duck-hooks. It's a mental thing. Lodged in some dark corner of his psyche there's a synaptic nerve-ending that ain't cutting the mustard. He's convinced he can't pee at a trough. In fact, he's become so aware of it now that he simply won't use them. He'd rather his bladder explode than risk the embarrassment of another no-show at crunch-time.

One time while a group of us were out on the town, one of the guys came back from the men's room with a tremendous grin on his face and proudly announced the bathroom had a trough. All eyes turned to Schlep. Schlep promptly offered a few choice expletives and turned his attention to his beer. We figured he could hold out for maybe an hour before Mother Nature began pounding on the door. It was actually closer to two hours and we all marvelled at Schlep's will-power. We even benefitted from a free round of beers bought by a nearby table after Schlep impressed them with his moves on the dance floor. Of course if they only knew the reason behind his footwork and contortions they probably wouldn't have offered a liquid reward. Finally Schlep gave in, but instead of risking public humiliation he opted for plan-B: the trusty parking lot. That's one of the beauties of being a guy. We don't necessarily need a bathroom, a shrub will do nicely, thank you. But being that there were no shrubs handy Schlep used an old beat-up hubcap. That would have been fine and dandy except the hubcap was still connected to a Camaro and the owner happened to be inside the car giving a physical to some sweet young thing he had lured from the bar. The guy, who had the dimensions of a front-loader, quickly popped his head out the window. At least we were pretty sure it was his head. It was located above his shoulders in spite of the fact no neck was visible.

A recent, unscientific study performed by the authors of this fine literature determined that on the average it takes somewhere in the neighborhood of eleven-point-three-seconds to empty a full bladder. Being that Schlep was only about two-seconds into his handywork, he still had a good nine-seconds of beer to expel from his body. That's hard enough to do standing still, but taking a leak in a dead sprint requires more dexterity and concentration than you'd imagine. Leaping fire hydrants and parking barriers just added to the level of difficulty. We knew that if he survived he would have received high marks indeed.

With the human front-loader hot at his heels we knew Schlep was done for, and I quietly collected my bets. But Schlep, in a desperate way, made a quick spin, and as luck would have it, he still had a good schooner's worth left in him, which immediately found its way across the front-loader's midriff.

The laws of physics apparently didn't apply that night, because everyone knows that large masses travelling at high rates of speed do not stop in millionths of a second. This mass, however, did. The mass also began his own peculiar dance, all the while slapping at the dark trail across his abdomen, and emitting a high-pitched squeal.

Schlep didn't need a second opinion. He was shook-off, zipped-up and gone in a blur. No dummies, we figured guilt by association was enough to send the front-loader in our direction so we beat a hasty retreat as well.

I was thinking, there must be a way to avoid these situations. And it occurred to me that when we go out, we buy beer, drink the beer and eventually the beer ends up in the toilet. I say, get rid of the middleman! Give me a beer to hold, but it's strictly for aestetics. Hell, it could just as soon be a glass of water with some yellow food coloring in it to set the right atmosphere. What we really need is a *"buzz-pill"*: a concentrated alcohol pill, to swallow so we don't actually have to drink the beer. This way I'd still get my buzz, I'd have a glass to hold so I woudn't look like a geek, standing around with my hands in my pockets, and when I'm tired of holding the glass I'd just pour the beer in the toilet. So much for stage fright! Ok, so maybe the *"buzz-pill"* might get abused a tad bit. That's what lawyers are for.

I think I've just figured out how I'm going to make my first million.

13
Male Strippers Make Women Weird

While working one summer on a fishing boat in Ketchikan, Alaska, a couple of the ship's deck hands and I went out on the town to sample the city's finer malt beverages. After a brisk stroll we happened upon one of the many drinking establishments and popped inside. As luck would have it this particular drinkery had a couple of bonuses going for it. For one, their list of beers easily tripled that of the average Alaskan dive. We could barely contain our excitement when we realized we could choose between Bud, Olympia *and* Pabst Blue Ribbon. After agonizing over the selection I finally opted for the king of beers. When the bartender popped the cap off the bottle for me, saving me the embarrassment of trying to impress my co-workers by removing the bottle cap with my eye socket, I immediately recognized this as a class establishment. The second dead giveaway was that there was a stage in the corner of the bar with a boombox sitting quietly on it. Ok, so maybe "*stage*" would be a bit presumptuous, but it sounded better than "*two stacks of pallets with some rotting plywood running between them*." Anytime you're in an Alaska bar with a stage that can only mean one thing: strippers. Of course, chances are if you're in *any* Alaska bar that means strippers.

It was a pretty good crowd for a Tuesday night. Dozens of fisherman filled the room with a good blend of revelry, small talk and baseball caps. At around nine o'clock a thin blonde waif pushed her way through the crowd and up to the "*stage*." She appeared to be about sixteen, going on thirty-five.

She popped a tape of some generic techno-pop artist in and began her show. At the time, I was just nineteen myself and had only witnessed a stripper a couple of times before at other Alaskan establishments. The reaction of the crowd never ceased to amaze me. The girl bumped and grinded half-heartedly for a few minutes to the rapt attention of the gathered horde. The men all watched and sipped their beers in quiet reverence. A few of the more drunken sailors gave a few lurid yelps and screams, but for the most part everyone was well-behaved. When the girl finished her show with a clever little move that indicated to me she must be lacking at least four vertebrae, the men clapped politely before resuming their conversations. As the girl wound her way through the crowd to the bathroom I could hear the patrons giving her warm congratulations on her performance.

If you walk into any given strip joint, chances are you'll see a similar reaction. Bachelor parties, however, are a bit different. Those have a tendency to be a bit more raucous. But even the most tawdry bachelor parties are nothing compared to what you'd see if you went to a place presenting "*The Men of Chippendales*," or, "*The Dream Machine*," or any of those other travelling male strip teams. The women on hand achieve a state of reckless euphoria and start yelling things I doubt you'd repeat to your mother. Of course, chances are your mother probably sat in on one of those exhibitions at one time or another.

They chant, hoot, scream, holler, beg, cajole and basically drop themselves at least three notches on the evolutionary chain. In other words, they act a lot like guys do during college basketball's final four weekend.

At one time in my existence I had the questionable pleasure of living in the thriving metropolis of Butte, Montana. On one of the many cold evenings a friend of mine informed me that one of those male dance troupes was swinging through town and that the bar they were performing at was looking for extra help for the night. Images of reckless women waving spare cash around circled my head and I promptly beat cheeks down to the pub to reserve my spot on the employment list.

The "*Fantasy Lads*" were scheduled to perform promptly at eight but by eight thirty they still hadn't shown up. Concern was etched fairly deep into the owner's forehead and the rest of us weren't exactly smiling up a storm either. The crowd had gone beyond restless. They were beginning to turn ugly. Or should I say *uglier*. The poor sap who drew the short straw and had to inform this angry mob that the lads were late never stood a chance. I'm still amazed by the display of dexterity it took for the four woman nearest the stage to reach up and drag the unlucky messenger, kicking and screaming, into the mob. The look of abject terror on his face as his head sank below the sea of hair-extensions will forever be emblazoned in my brain.

We'd managed to keep them fairly sedate with a constant flow of alcohol but the taps were beginning to run dry. We knew that it would only be a matter of time before things got out-of- hand. Sure, we'd probably take a few of them with us but their sheer numbers would prove to be an irresistible force that would crush us like bugs.

Two of the younger employees couldn't take the pressure and went screaming for the exits. The fools. That's just what the women wanted us to do. They never reached the doors. A wave of heavily made-up divorcees rained down upon them, as the hapless employees' shrieks for help bounced harmlessly across the beer-streaked floor.

Time was running out. I'd just witnessed a bevy of salon beauticians breaking up furniture to build sacrificial fires and realized that drastic measures were necessary. I collared the owner and screamed above the din into one of his large and decidely hairy ears, "The needs of the many outweigh the needs of the few!"

It took him a moment to recognize the reference. "Star Trek II: The Wrath of Khan, right? When Spock sacrificed himself to save the ship!" he bellowed back.

"Correct! I'm willing to be Spock!" I hollered just as one of the busboys was being tied to a stake and dowsed with a healthy serving of Bacardi one-fifty-one.

The owner clapped a calloused but affectionate hand on my shoulder and screamed back, "You're a good man! If you survive the night there's a free six-pack of Schmidt waiting for you!" At which point he dove over the bar just as a battalion of sorority girls turned the pool tables over like police cars in East L.A.

I rushed to the juke box, quickly inserted a quarter and punched in the number for (the artist formerly known as) Prince's "*Erotic City.*" As the first pulsing beats began to waft over the rioting masses I made a mad dash for the stage. For a brief moment I stared in stunned silence at the carnage laid before me. No furniture remained intact. Broken bottles were all the rage, and the smell of stale beer choked the air. Several clots of women dotted the lounge, each one engaged in some form of destructive revelry. A dozen or so former airline attendants were performing an assortment of grim experiments on one of the slower-footed waiters, while a gaggle of ladies from the local bowling lane were carrying on some sort of horrific ritual with the assistant manager.

I grabbed the mike and yelled something incomprehensible just as the slow-footed waiter was about to discover why people aren't normally fond of enemas. . .especially with pool cues.

I don't know why, but the place went strangely silent. I looked out amongst the wreckage to see all eyes on me. The only sound was the pulsing beat of Erotic City building up to the first spoken words of the song.

This was my cue.

"Ladies! It's the moment you've all been waiting for! The. . .uh. . .Fantasy Lad!" I prayed to whichever gods were present that the women hadn't noticed "*Lads*," had become "*Lad*." At which point I did a complete three-sixty grabbed my crotch a gave my best pelvic thrust.

The ladies dropped who they were doing and rushed forward like a swarm of locusts. Ok, so I'm not six two, two hundred pounds of rippling meat. By that point in the evening, Mister French from Family Affair could have been peeling his garb and they wouldn't have cared a lick.

I went through the standard moves, kicking off my shoes, tossing my sweaty socks into the crowd, pumping my lower extremities furiously, all the while running my hands through my hair and brandishing a look of orgasmic exaltation. One stupendously overweight housewife somehow managed to leap up onto the stage and for a brief moment I saw myself meeting a sudden and very messy death but thankfully she only wanted to plant a sloppy, wet kiss on me. Before I managed to fend her off I was beginning to think maybe being crushed to death would have been more pleasant.

I peeled and pumped all the way down to my Fruit of the Looms, while the women randomly charged the stage only to be beaten down by their compatriots who didn't want to have their view obstructed. A sea of dollar bills waved before me like wheat on the eve of harvest. And it was a bumper crop, I might add. I plucked the bills diligently and even dropped down to my knees to let a few of the lucky ones stuff their currency into my skivies.

I began to recognize the decaying last notes of the song and realized that prudence was the better part of valor. It was time to make my escape.

I dragged my prone body across the stage in mock

sexual delight and as soon as I was behind the curtains I gathered up what remaining clothes I could find off stage and made a break for the rear door, the cheers of the crowd flowing out into the night air as I scampered to freedom.

I'm not sure what happened inside after I left. I felt I'd given the employees plenty of time to beat a hasty retreat and had managed to make myself a few bucks in the deal. I heard that once the women realized no one else was going to take the stage and that there were no more employees to torment they set torches to the bar and danced around the building like it was some sort of pagan funeral pyre.

Hmmm. I wonder what the deductible is on male stripper insurance?

14
Of Boob Jobs and Astro-Turf

When you're a kid you always dream of playing football on astro-turf. You grew up playing on grass, dirt, and pavement, so the idea of catching a deep bomb on astro-turf seemed absolutely exotic--so big-league! I remember going to high-school games when I was about twelve and thinking, "*Wow, what a cool field. Astro-turf!*" The fact that probably every player on that field was thinking, "*Lousy carpet. We might as well be playing on concrete!*" never occurred to me. Of course, I'd never been tackled on astro-turf. Everyone loves astro-turf till they're tackled on it. Nothing like a nine-inch carpet burn that takes seven weeks to heal and several painful nights of having the sheets stick to your wounds and tear them open every time you roll over to take the charm out of something.

I still remember the first time I played on turf. Several buddies and had I snuck over the barbed wire at the local high-school stadium and threw the pigskin around. It was approximately one second after Spanky Peznick drilled me into the carpet that I realized that astro-turf was evil. Instead of nice, soft, forgiving grass to break my fall I landed on this nightmarish green slab of granite that proceeded to peel the flesh from my body. Now that I've grown up and learned more of the subtlties of the sporting events I love I'm a true advocate of grass fields. Astro-turf may look nice, be low maintenance and last a long time but it's lousy to play on.

The same goes for fake boobs.

Women in general seem to be pretty insecure about their breasts. This, of course is a result of "*society*," they tell me. "*The media*" is another good scapegoat. TV and magazines show all these D-cup babes and the B-cup women of the world figure that's all men want. A car-fanatic buddy of mine once said in reference to engines, "*There is no substitute for cubic inches*." I'm sure women figure guys feel the same way about breasts. Of course I'd bet the farm that more than a few women have made the same crass comment about certain male body parts too. The truth is that guys *do* dig women's breasts. But they don't have to be of goliath proportions, they just have to be nice. Of course if they're big *and* nice, all the better. But big isn't always nice. Case in point: Fake boobs.

One time I was sitting by a pool on a particularly sweltering summer day when this woman with what could only be described as a tremendous body happened by. I tried not to stare but it was useless. This of course didn't sit terribly well with my girlfriend at the time, as the sharp dig to my ribs indicated.

"They're fake, you know."

"Excuse me?" I countered, knowing full well this was a conversation that was headed for a poor conclusion.

"Those boobs were bought and paid for."

At this point I gave a response that women hate but most guys would tend to agree with. "Who cares?" I said.

The glare that followed promptly wilted all the vegetation around my chair and didn't do much for me either. I still stand by that comment though. Who cares if they're fake? I'm just a guy taking in the sights. They look tremendous, and it feels good to look at them. This, of course, is where fake boobs and astro-turf take on similar characteristics.

Until recently I'd never dated a woman with fake boobs. In fact, I wasn't even aware, at first, that she'd gone under the knife. She'd always had a nice body and usually made a point to show it off. I guess she just wanted a little extra volume. As I'd indicated before, from a sightseeing perspective they were wonderful, but that wonderment came to a screeching halt the moment I laid a hand on one breast. In an instant I knew, "*fake boob*!" There I was, trying to act casual and continue a particularly nice kiss and all I could think was, "*fake boob*!" Let me tell you, it's no small task trying to hold up your end of a good old-fashioned tongue wag when your mind is focused approximately eight inches lower. You begin making comparisons immediately.

"*Hmm, they're awfully firm,*" I'm thinking, "*they don't give as much as normal ones.*"

I was hoping the woman just assumed I was feeling her up instead of doing a physical analysis of her breasts. But this was fascinating stuff--a new experience! "*I must do more research!*" I thought, and quickly shifted over to the left breast.

"*Hmm, interesting. Extremely similar to the right breast. A general lack in softness and elasticity. Pressure exerted by thumb and forefinger yield negligible amounts of give. Move on to exertion of force from the side. Hmm, fake breasts are more pliant when force is applied in a lateral fashion instead of the standard front-lift approach.*"

You must remember that this was all racing through my mind while straddling a gear-shift knob in the front seat of her Honda Accord in a deserted parking lot.

As I'd alluded to earlier, guys *not* dating a woman with fake boobs have absolutely no problem with the the whole fake boob thing. Of course, chances are most guys dating a woman with fake-o's aren't gonna whine too much either. However, there is one thing he must learn to deal with, simply, that everyone else, men and women alike, will be staring at his doll's snug top.

Before he ever began dating the fake-boob woman it was he who was doing the staring. When he viewed, the standard thoughts that went through his head were "*Wow!*" or maybe, "*Could those be real?*" or, "*Who is the lucky, lucky man who knows the secret behind that blouse?*" And of course maybe "*Wow!*" again.

He must also learn to deal with the fact that his buddies are going to take more of an interest in hanging out with him . . .and his girlfriend, than in the past. He'll notice that all of a sudden his friends are inviting him. . .

and his girlfriend, to the beach or hot-tubbing, or any place else that her breasts will be on display more than normal.

She won't mind either. It's a guarantee that she got the boob job for a reason. . .so she, and they, would look good. And don't think she's not about to put the spotlight on them occasionally. Those babies cost cash--lot's of it. They aren't about to be hidden away in the closet like an old set of golf clubs.

OK. We all know about the fake boob thing, so for the sake of fairness, let's take a brief look at the male counterpart. Have any of you seen the ads that pop up on the sports page touting the virtues of penile enlargement? Typically, they're found below an ad for the bald guy needing a new lid.

Is this type of surgery strictly for the guy to help satisfy his woman? I doubt it. Suppose he doesn't have a woman? I can't see him sitting at the bar striking up small talk with the redhead beside him with this little bit of ammo in his sales kit.

"*Hi, my name's Bart. You know those ads for Ball Park franks? About how they plump when you cook em*?"

Sorry. Can't see it. Guys may go out with an ugly woman if she's got nice hooters but most women won't give an ugly guy the time of day, regardless of the cubic inches he's sporting below the belt.

So if it ain't strictly for scoring with babes, why else? Perhaps for the casual stroll through the locker room or the time he and "*Big Johnny*" are relaxing in the steam room. Just another guy ego thing, I suppose.

When women get fake boobs you know damn well she's gonna want to show them off to her friends. She'll give them all good looks, maybe even some pokes, prods and touches. Call me wacky, but I don't think you'll see a guy who just went under the knife, whippin' out "*Mister Happy*" and inviting his pals to get a closer inspection. What he'd likely get is a few more swollen body parts.

15
The Bar Scene

Life in your early twenties is a great time, filled with high entertainment, pursued with reckless abandon. But God made sure to keep things in check by imbuing us with several negative personality traits during this portion of life. Sadly, there's not much that can be done about it. It's a genetic imperative that's only affected by time. God was sharp enough to make sure that by our early twenties we'd still have a bit of teen-age residue imprinted on our DNA. It's that residue that instills the false belief we know everything, and that we're bulletproof. Luckily this residue fades, otherwise, we'd be cursed to walk the earth oblivious to our surroundings and pissing people off.

Everyone knows teenagers are obnoxious by nature so they're tolerated. But for some unknown reason we seem to think once a person hits the magic 2-1 everything changes, that they somehow instantaneously become responsible. Yeah, right. Hold your thumb and forefinger about half an inch apart; that's the maturity difference between an eighteen year old and a twenty one year old. Just because they can drink cheap hooch without having to sneak it from their dad's liquor cabinet doesn't mean squat. Go to a typical singles bar for the barely legal set and you'll see what I mean.

I firmly believe that when people in their early twenties are drinking in a bar they tend to forget they're in public view. I spent eighteen months spinning records (back when they were records) at a suburban lounge. You know the place; the bar has a dance floor roughly the size of a postage stamp and the DJ isn't allowed to turn the music up beyond a whisper until after ten because it will keep Mister and Misses Whitebread America from digesting their meatloaf in the adjoining restaurant. It was one of those places that became strangely popular because the suburbanite youth didn't want to drive all the way downtown, and it was close enough to their parents' house (where they're still living) so they could weave drunkenly down back streets to get home. The music was strictly Top Fourty, and after midnight so were the IQ's.

Over the months, it wasn't tough to notice several consistencies in behavioral patterns. The first of which I like to call "the walk of death." Since every guy who has been shot down by a girl has made "the walk of death," let me describe to you a typical "walk of death" scenario. (Guys, if you think reading this may result in a "walk of *death"* flashback, please skip to the next page.)

From my perch in the DJ booth I had an exceptionately good view of the evening's revelers, and throughout the night I noticed one particular goddess who was turning guys down at an alarming rate. It was like watching a squadron of Zeros swarming down on a heavily armed battleship. But there was too much flak and the Zeros, one at a time, spiralled into the drink. It didn't take a genius to see she was an untouchable. Of course, that's never stopped guys before. Our masochist gland kicks in and we gamely make our futile efforts. I noticed one such lad was seated in the far corner of the bar, eyeing the exotic beauty, and recognized immediately that he was going to make an effort. It made me cringe.

"Don't do it, pal," I thought. *"She's got her deflector shields up."*

Of course, from thirty feet away he couldn't hear my thoughts; took one last swill of his gin and tonic and boldly went forth. It was like that moment right before you're in a horrible car accident and everything feels like it's happening in slow motion. You can see it all unfolding in front of you and yet you're helpless to stop it. I could only look on, empathizing with what he would be feeling within a matter of moments.

He hovered near her table, waiting patiently for the throbbing beats of some Billy Ocean tune to subside before making his play. For my part I tossed on a popular Madonna tune, hoping even she couldn't turn that down, but I knew better. You see, as it clearly states in the *guy handbook,* once a woman has turned one guy down she can't exactly hop on the floor with the next guy who comes along. Her name and ancestry would be bludgeoned, reviled and generally trod-upon by the poor sap who got the earlier thumbs down.

The guy waited a few beats to see if it was a worthy song and made his attempt. Mercifully, it went smoothly and by the numbers. A clean death, taking no more than a few seconds. Hopefully he was sufficiently anaesthetized beforehand. He asked, she said no dice and he then began the arduous "*walk of death.*" The space that he crossed from his table to hers was no more than twenty five feet, and that distance can be traversed at a comfortable pace in approximately seven seconds. But that same walk going back with your tail between your legs takes an eternity. I would imagine it has something to do with the fact it's not as easy swaggering, and trying to not look like an undesirable loser who just went down in a ball of flames. Of course, the closer you are to twenty one and the more drunk you are, the easier "*the walk of death*" is. You're more fearless and really don't give a rip that some stupid bimbo, whom you really didn't want to dance with anyway, decided that she just came to the lounge to listen to music. So there. That's one thing we guys have going for us; the God-given gift of rationalization. Women analyze, men rationalize. We always can come up with some reason why we do something stupid or something stupid happens to us. My buddy Otis Hamhand is the master of rationalization. He gets suckered into buying some dumb-ass Veg-o-matic on a late-night infomercial and then tries to convince anyone who will listen that he's been seriously considering becoming a vegetarian for well over a year now and he'd finally decided to take the plunge. We all nod accordingly and try not to smirk when we see the, still-boxed, Veg-o-matic selling for a buck-fifty at his next garage sale. But I digress, let's get back to the bar.

Another thing I would regularly witness is "*the oblivious couple.*" This is the pair who become so transfixed with each other they forget there are other people in the room. One particularly dead Tuesday night I noticed a guy picking up on one of the three or four single women who dotted the room. One hour and three firm bourbon and sevens later they were well into giving each other complete physicals. While playing one of my token slow songs for the evening, the four couples who made up the bulk of the crowd held court on the dance floor. When the song ended everyone made their way back to their respective tables. . .except our own couple number one: "*The oblivious couple.*"

They were locked in what would normally pass for a battle of survival on Mutual of Omaha's Wild Kingdom. But on this night, we'll just call it shameless groping. There they were in the middle of the dance floor, a rain of colored lights dancing over their intertwined bodies. For everyone else in the bar it was one of those situations where you know you shouldn't watch, but you have to. This lust-fest went on for a good sixty seconds, which doesn't sound like very long but feels like a millennium, because of the *can't watch/must watch* dilemma.

While watching the nightly hormone frenzy, I noticed there are certain truths that cannot be ignored by anyone with an ounce of common sense. One of these truths applies to asking women to dance. If you've got your eye on a girl who's with several of her friends you'd better be damn certain she's gonna want to dance with you or the whole table will be shot. If you get denied and then are stupid enough to ask the girl sitting next to her, basically what she will be hearing is, "*Hi, your much more attractive friend was unwilling to cooperate so would you like to play the role of second-round draft choice?"* If you walk away without wearing a beverage consider yourself blessed.

Another thing that never ceased to amaze me was the geniuses who would hit on a woman obviously waiting for someone to meet her. These rockheads seem to think it's completely natural for an astoundingly beautiful woman to walk into a bar by herself. Sorry, boys, but I think someone at the asylum misinformed you.

One night I was with several buds, tipping some cold ones, when a vision entered the bar. Every guy in the place took heed as she settled into an empty booth, and one of my slower pals immediately piped up, "Look who's coming to dinner!"

The rest of us smiled at his naivete, like a grandfather watching his excitable six year old grandson in a toy store.

"Dude, she's obviously waiting for someone. And judging by her looks, ten bucks says it's her boyfriend," I reminded him. "Women who look like that almost always have boyfriends--big ones who frequently play middle linebacker for professional sports franchises."

He wasn't convinced. "C'mon. You can't pass up a dish like that. Somebody's gotta make a play!"

"Fine." I said, "Go over there and use that Errol Flynn charm of yours and sweep her off her feet. We'll come over and sweep up your pieces when her boyfriend shows up."

Apparently the one common-sense nerve-ending he does possess fired and he wisely held his ground. Sure enough, ten minutes later a perfectly chiseled guy walked in and took up residence next to the babe. He was one of those strong-jawed men with the annoying habit of having an upper body in the shape of an inverted triangle. Guys like that irritate the hell out of me.

One of the worse things about singles bars is if you happen to be at one, single. By that I mean by yourself. When you're solo you have no support team and are forced to look to yourself for strength. I don't think women fully appreciate this scenario, because they're usually smart enough to avoid having it happen.

One time, while out with the crew, one of the women at our table sneered over at the wall of single guys hanging out. "Look at those guys. Just looking for someone to swoop on. They're pathetic."

"Hey!" I snapped. "I've been one of those guys. Trust me, it sucks." Obviously she was in need of guy education. And when last I checked, my teaching certificate was still in order. School was now in session.

"You think those guys are enjoying themselves? Ha! Fat chance," I snorted. "They're nervous, uncomfortable, and wishing to God they had a buddy right now."

I flashed back to those moments when I'd found myself hanging out in a bar waiting for a pal to show up, sitting there, feeling like "*Lord Spaz on high*." It was particularly annoying because only an hour earlier I was indestructible.

It's always the same; before you leave the house you're all fired up, telling yourself how the world is your oyster and before you lies the great unknown. You're fearless, you're motivated, you're God! Expectations are running high and your personality toggle switch is in the "*on*" position. Of course, more often than not, the moment you show up at the bar and you find yourself waiting for your buds, reality comes crashing down like a sack of spuds. Your confidence shrivels up like diseased walnuts, and your *motivation* undergoes a sex-change operation and suddenly turns into *desperation.*

First of all, there's an outstanding chance your buds are gonna dog you, cuz that's just what guys do. So you immediately rush to the bar to get something in your hand, otherwise you look like twice the geek standing around with your arms crossed, or worse yet, hanging at your sides. For some reason you don't feel quite so stupid standing by yourself when you've got a drink in your hand. You are then forced to assume the position of the guy trying to look nonchalant. Failure is imminent because it's impossible to look nonchalant when you're trying to look nonchalant.

You stand in any available space, preferably leaning (it helps with the nonchalant bit) and nurse your beer. Your eyes dart around the room, desperately hoping you'll find eye contact, because eye contact is the saviour. Once eye contact is achieved you then have an opportunity to at least try to strike up conversation. At which point you can stop leaning and bag the nonchalant routine. At least until you find out the eye contact was an accident and you're forced to make, "*the walk of death,*" back to your starting position. You then make a few token comments to the equally uncomfortable guy next to you, but that's all. You're not there to get cozy with some loser who's in the same boat as you, you're there panning for gold! The bar is your river bed and word is that many a miner has struck it rich here. Of course, if everything goes by the books, by midnight your wallet will be empty and your pan will be full. . .of rocks. Oh sure, during the course of the evening you'll have thought you'd uncovered a few nuggets; thought you were making time, only to find out that you were just being played for a sap--fools gold!

By the time I'd finished educating the girl on the subtlties and nuances of bar-prospecting she seemed adequately humbled; or so I thought. Five minutes later she was suckering some poor fool with fake eye contact. Just another hapless miner lured by the thrill of instant riches.

16
Speaking in Metaphors

Guys have never been accused of being communication specialists. . .according to women. Personally, I have never had a problem deciphering a message from another guy. The words always seemed clear, straightforward and to the point. When two men are talking there never seems to be any of that annoying circling the issue we save for our discussions with women or that women save for men. Of course, there's usually an underlying reason for that: Men want to be clear with other men. It's expected. Whereas, men don't really care if they're clear with women. That, too, is expected.

If men want to discuss something and don't feel like whispering like snivelling wieners they'll speak in a way that makes it hard for someone else to understand. It's like when you're visiting your second cousin Balthazar in the tiny European hamlet of Dorkburg; the local inhabitants will act like they don't speak English when in fact they damn well speak it fluently. This way they can listen in on your conversations and know precisely what you're talking about. It only takes a couple of embarrassing international incidents to wise you up. So what do you do? You put your years of adolescence to good use and start speaking in extreme American slang. Pity the poor Euro-sap who tries to decipher this conversation.

Ugly American 1: Yo, what say we treb to your pad and hang for a spell.

Ugly American 2: Cool. You got scarfable chow?

They'd zap a neuron or two trying to make heads or tails of that exchange. Guys will do approximately the same thing back at home but instead of standard slang, we'll use sports metaphors. We don't necessarily do it to annoy women, that just happens to be a bonus side effect.

Speaking in sports metaphors is extremely handy for guys. Great for the ego, too. It makes us feel like we can actually speak a second language. Let me show you. The following example would be a discussion between two guys concerning another guy who was trying to meet a woman but whimped out. (Translation in parenthesis following each comment.)

Dude 1:   He choked, bigger than life. *(He squandered an opportunity.)*

Dude 2:   A severe Seattle Super Sonic first-round choke. But he had no game plan! He stepped to the plate, missed the signals and ended up dragging his pathetic butt back to the dug-out with the wood still rooted to his shoulder. *(Most definitely. Similar to the Seattle basketball franchise which performed admirably during the regular season, only to be ousted from the playoffs in a most unceremonious manner. He was certainly ill-prepared to handle the situation. He underestimated her interest in him and gave up without trying.)*

Dude 1:   That was one of the weakest at-bats I've ever witnessed. The guy didn't even take his cuts! *(That was, indeed, a poor attempt.)*

Dude 2:   No kidding. If that were me I'd be swinging for the cheap-seats. I may end up sitting next to him in the dug-out but I'll be damned if I don't foul off a few before I take a seat. *(Truly. Had it been me in a similar circumstance I would have given it the old college try. My attempt may have proven futile, but not for lack of effort.)*

Dude 1:   Seriously! And she was live! She was serving up meatballs and he went down looking. The ball was in his court, for crying out loud! He could have spotted up for a trey, instead he decides to burn the clock, turns it over and ends up riding the pine instead. *(Quite so. And it appeared she was interested. Her actions were certainly of a flirtatious nature, but he appeared not to notice. I'm certain he could have secured a future meeting with her but he hesitated, and thus his endeavors resulted in failure.)*

Dude 2:   Did he take it strong to the hole? No, he weaseled out and ends up feeding someone else. You can't score if you don't have the rock! *(Had he taken a more dynamic approach there is a high probability that it would be himself enjoying her company instead of that other gentleman who is currently occupying her time. You certainly cannot succeed without giving yourself the appropriate opportunity in which to do so.)*

Clearer now? You'll note in the final comments the sudden and unexpected transition to another sport (baseball to basketball). To the true "*guy*" this is of no concern. He simply punches the clutch and drops it into another gear. Oops. See what I mean?

I've often wondered if women speak in metaphors about men. If they did it would probably be in clothes or shopping terms.

<u>Girl 1</u>: Did you see that guy by the drinking fountain? He was anything but off-the-rack!

<u>Girl 2</u>: Oh puh-leaze! You'd break out the card for that? He was a second if ever I saw one. Strictly Ross-for-less.

<u>Girl 1</u>: Honey, what do you know about men? I've seen your dates. You talk rayon and settle for burlap. That last guy you were with was definitely on the clearance table!

<u>Girl 2</u>: At least he wasn't as high-maintenance as your last boyfriend. Sure, the guy was silk but how much of your time was spent at the drycleaners? You constantly had the iron on for him. Give me a good cotton-blend man any day.

<u>Girl 1</u>: Yeah, I see your point. But it seems like all the good merchandise has been picked over. Everything on the shelves has either been returned because it's flawed or clashes with everything I have.

<u>Girl 2</u>: Yeah. But I keep hoping sooner or later I'll find that perfect fit in just the right colors, wrinkle free!

<u>Girl 1</u>: Sure. And at fifty percent off retail.

<u>Girl 2</u>: A girl can dream, can't she?

17
The Amalgam

People ask me what I'm looking for in a potential wife. That's simple. I'm looking for the perfect woman. Of course, since there's no such thing as the perfect woman then I'll just have to be content with a woman who's perfect for me. Actually, what I, like every other person on the planet am looking for, is an amalgam: a combination of the best parts of several people you admire or lust after.

The woman who cuts my hair (hairdresser is too weenie a term for guys to use) told me she would be happy with three men: one who brings home the bacon, one who's a domestic dynamo and one chained in the basement for sex. You want stimulating conversation, you go out with bacon-guy and discuss theatre. If you're tired and just want a comfortable snuggle on the couch while watching Melrose Place, you collar domestic-man. You want some action, you cruise to the basement and grunt with Homer for a few rounds. Sounds pretty good.

How many times have you and your buds sat around and said, "*If I could take Lisa's face and Charlotte's bod and Inga's personality. . .*"

Of course this isn't a conversation you can share honestly and freely with your significant other. You even open your mouth one centimeter about such a shallow thought and it's curtains. Unless you're dating Elle Macpherson chances are that sooner or later your girlfriend will be paging through your Sports Illustrated swimsuit issue, with a somewhat knitted brow, and finally hold up a picture of some perfectly formed buxom goddess and ask the fatal question: "Do you wish I had boobs like that?"

She might as well ask, "Do you wish you had more money than God?"

This reminds me of the second Star Trek movie, which opened with Kirstie Alley piloting the USS Kobiashi Maru through an impossible situation. Surrounded by Klingons, the ship was doomed. It was an exercise known as the "*no-win scenario.*" When your girlfriend asks you if you wish she had boobs like a Sports Illustrated swimsuit model you too have entered the world of the "*no-win scenario.*" At this point your options are limited. You can try acting like you didn't hear the question, because she feels you don't listen anyway, or you could say you could have sworn you heard the phone ring and dash out of the room. Chances are though, you're screwed and have to buck up. . .and lie like a dog. "Are you kidding? You're perfect just the way you are!"

You then promptly hide behind your sports page before she notices that your nose just grew four inches.

The amalgam would be that perfect blend of Betty and Veronica: the gorgeous babe who can hang with the guys; the woman who's a financial wizard, a dancing fool, an avid sports fan, a doting mother, can cook like Betty Crocker and who's a slut in the bedroom. Where are you, oh girl of my dreams?

Trying to find the amalgam is also a no-win scenario. You find something good but you want something great. Nothing like good old-fashioned greed to mess things up. It's like driving downtown when you stumble across a parking place three blocks from where you're going. You stupidly think, "*Heck, I'll find a closer spot.*" And a half hour later you're picking your tongue off the pavement after you just hiked twenty seven blocks from the parking space you eventually found.

Me and my buddy Dweeb Thingus were out shooting pool at "*Oregon Slim's House of Pool,*" named after that billiards near-legend "*Oregon Slim,*" who would have crossed over from near-legend to legend if it wasn't for the incident concerning that trick shot with the blindfold, meat-cleavers and Dalmation puppy that went awry. I'm sure you read about it in the papers.

At any rate, Dweeb and I were on table five, enjoying a good game of "*miss the pockets,*" our favorite and easily most proficient game, when a stunning beauty came sauntering by and flashed Dweeb "*the look.*" It's tough to miss "*the look.*" If "*the look*" had a sound it could easily be mistaken for "*Psst. Over here, dummy!*"

Of course, if you've got a translator and it's wired for "*the look*," it could also sound like, "*Take me, I'm yours. Let's do it tonight! Let me be your love slave.*"

Luckily it was Dweeb and not Nob, "*the human party favor*," who was with me that night or it could have gotten ugly. Dweeb merely shrugged off "*the look*" like he got it all the time, and lined up his next miss.

"Uh, Dweeb. You just got '*the look*,' in case you hadn't noticed."

"Yeah. I saw." Dweeb answered indifferently as he succeeded in pulling off a perfectly executed miss of the three ball that was two inches from the pocket.

"Aren't you gonna follow it up?'

"Nah. Not interested."

I was so shook by this startling reply that I inadvertently made a two-bank combination shot that dropped the two, seven and nine balls respectively.

"And just why are you not interested? She was a babe! Get your ass over there right now!"

"Her ankles looked kind of big. That's the support structure. You figure if she's got big ankles now who knows what the rest of her could balloon up to somewhere down the line."

I was stunned. So stunned my next shot curled magically around the eight ball and softly clipped the twelve ball which then rolled through an impossibly small opening and dropped into the corner pocket. My flustered shots were beginning to attract an audience; a group of fifteen or twenty onlookers who no doubt play the silly version of billiards where you actually try to knock the balls in. I'd tried it before but found my style much more suited to the under-appreciated game that

Dweeb and I have mastered of keeping the balls on the table.

"Big ankles? She was a total babe! A gorgeous face, a great bod! She was ninety-percent pure!"

Dweeb didn't seem to mind my blustering. He was too busy being embarrassed by my sudden affinity for knocking balls in with any manner of angle or combination. I'm sure the applause wasn't helping any either.

"Of course, if she had the ankles of that doll on table three, I'd be all over her."

Now it was I who was embarrassed--and infuriated! Opportunity doesn't knock nearly enough and here it was whacking on his door. To hide my red face I quickly sent the cue ball in the exact opposite direction of every ball on the table in an attempt to regain my pool prowess. I was apparently more distraught than I imagined. The cue ball took a crazy spin, bounced back, hopped over one ball, negotiated through a couple of enemy balls and gave the fifteen ball the perfect touch to send it dropping into the side pocket. Never had I shot so poorly. When the onlookers began asking for pointers and autographs I found myself too concerned about Dweeb's indifference to the babe and waved them off. For some strange reason this only seemed to encourage them. More gathered around the table as my game continued to falter and more balls fell. Above the cheering I yelled to Dweeb, "Let's get out of here. I can't play with all these distractions; and you're too stupid to know what's good for you!"

We left the fawning billiard wannabes and made a bee-line for the door. We passed the babe who proceeded to give Dweeb a second rendition of "*the look*;" all Dweeb did was glance at her ankles, and look longingly back at the support system of the girl on table three.

Just think; if Dweeb hadn't been so picky and wasn't looking for the amalgam, he might have a babe to call his own and I'd still be able to play "*miss the pockets*," at Oregon Slim's. I can't shoot there anymore, it's too embarrassing--especially since they bronzed my cue and hung that portrait of me over table five.

18
The Glance

You've read about "*stage fright*," now I think you're ready for another guy thing that's normally kept quiet. It doesn't really have a name but for now we'll just call it "*the glance*." Like it's better-known brother "*stage fright*," "*the glance*" also takes place in public restrooms in that arena of humiliation known as the urinal.

To look or not to look. That is the question. Look at what? Don't be stupid, you know exactly what I'm talking about. That piece of organic matter in your neighbor's hands for which the restroom was built.

Actually, if you're gonna look you better have peripheral vision rivaling a peregrine falcon, or you risk absorbing a withering stare and perhaps even a roundhouse right aimed at the soft spot behind your temple.

Everyone knows you're not supposed to look. It's like cheating on a test. You may have burned the midnight oil and studied like your beer money depended on it, but sometimes you find your eyes wandering aimlessly and accidentally catch a glimpse of your neighbor's answers. You didn't plan on it, it just sort of happened. But now it's a moot point. You've glanced, and now you have to see if their answers measure up to yours. It's kind of a genetic imperative. Trying not to look is not an option. I suppose with a superhuman burst of will-power and an iron constitution, you could keep your eyes focused on your own answers but there's a ninety percent chance you'd be using up your concentration reserves on this effort and trying to finish the rest of the test would be an exercise in futility.

When it comes to "*the glance*," doctors recommend you just give in, and look. Trying not to look has been known to result in medical catastrophe! Blood vessels weren't made to withstand that kind of pressure. When God put this package known as the human body together he just sort of figured that when the situation arose, we'd look. Of course, he didn't anticipate Eve suckering Adam into chomping the apple, resulting in all sorts of nasty emotional side effects, like pride, and embarrassment; emotions that twist our feeble minds into trying not to look when in fact we really want to look! So there you have it. Try not to look and risk a debilitating aneurism. It's not worth it.

How do you spot the guys coming out of the bathroom who've looked? Well, it's actually pretty easy. Chances are they're the ones coming out whistling nervously, shuffling their feet and trying to avoid any form of eye-contact. These are also the signs of urinal stage fright victims, but don't be fooled. There is one dead giveaway for spotting "*lookers.*" They're the ones rubbing the back of their necks. What usually happens is you're standing there and you glance down and accidentally catch a glimpse of your neighbor. Your brain's emergency system kicks in and internal alarms begin sounding in your head. This all takes place in the span of .003 seconds but it's long enough for you to realize that you've glanced and have to immediately look like you didn't glance. At this point you snap your head away in an effort to appear like you weren't looking, and in the process dislodge the upper portion of your spinal cord.

So, what do you do if you're caught in mid-glance? There are several options at your disposal. The first and most widely used option is to simply act like you didn't see anything. It's feeble, I know, but it's usually effective. Look impassive, that's the key. Don't frown, don't look shocked, and above all, don't crack a smile, no matter how small the guy's equipment is. You turn your gaze back to the tile wall at hand, shake, zip and go.

Another option you can explore is the old "*Hey, nice ring!*" ploy. Of course, if the guy isn't wearing a ring (on his finger, mind you) that sort of shoots that one down. At that point you may have to resort to plan-C, also known as the, "*lie like the pathetic dog that you are*" ploy. Plan-C is usually a last-ditch effort, but it's success rate of keeping one's teeth in one's mouth has been documented at eighty fourt percent.

Plan-C works like this: You've been caught in mid-glance, the guy's not wearing a ring, you already tried snapping your head away, but he ain't buying it. You can feel his steely gaze boring a gopher-hole through your head before the inevitable words come forth. "You some kinda faggot'r somethin'?"

Stay calm. Act surprised, like you didn't know he was addressing you, and paste on your most sincere smile.

"Who, me?" you grin.

"Yeah, you. I saw you lookin' at muh dick," is usually the type of high-brow comment you can expect.

"No, no, I wasn't looking at you. I was just doing a bit of homework. I actually work in research and development for American Standard toilets." At this point use your free hand like you're searching for your business card. "Ceramic is our staple but porcelain is our pride!"

This should take your neighbor mentally back a step before you continue on.

"Our most common urinal complaint is that the lip isn't big enough and as a result shoes are getting a shower. As we in the toilet industry like to say, 'That's enough to piss you off!' Har, har har."

This is about the point where your neighbor looks down and studies the urinal lip and nods his agreement. You're pretty well off the hook by now, but, to be safe, it's not a bad idea to give the guy's ego a boost, just for good measure.

"And I can see that with guys like you, it appears we'll have to make special urinals with an extra long lip since you obviously have to stand farther away than most men of normal proportions."

Consider the matter closed. He's probably checking out his proportions right about then and by the time a proper response has penetrated his under-used cerebral cortex you should be eight steps out the swinging door.

"*The glance*" is inevitable. Let's face it, you can stare at tile for only so long. If you haven't been caught glancing, you will. It's like death and taxes, only more embarrassing. Just remember, have a contingency plan and you'll never have to worry about where your wandering eyes may land. Of course, it wouldn't hurt to stand next to guys smaller than you.

19
The No Pride Club

I can say, with virtually no pride whatsoever, that I am a member of the NO PRIDE CLUB. It's easy to become a member, the only requirement is that you have a penis. In fact, our official club slogan is, *"All our members have members!"* Except for maybe priests, rabbis and other men of the cloth, all men are members of the NO PRIDE CLUB.

There are several cute sayings that try to sum up the NO PRIDE CLUB. One being, "*the little head thinking for the big head.*" But no one captured the epitome of the NO PRIDE CLUB like New York punk icon, Iggy Pop, when he crooned, "*While searching for a meaningful embrace, sometimes my self-respect took second place.*" Nuff said.

Being part of this brotherhood of shame isn't without reward though. The best reward being when you witness one of your co-members engaging in the privileges of membership (i.e.: hitting on a really drunk/ugly woman).

There was one time when several of my friends and I were out at some suburban dance dive, the "*Shangri-lounge*" I believe it was called, when we found ourselves having a heck of a time getting anybody to dance with us. We were a combined 0 for 12; a definite slump in anybody's book. Maybe it was the beer talking, but suddenly out of nowhere, my buddy Dweeb Thingus blurted fourth an astoundingly coherent suggestion.

"Since tonight we seem to be wearing the giant glowing "*L*" for "*Loser*", let's make the best of it. If we're gonna be losers, let's be phenomenal losers. Let's take loser to another level. Let's see who can be the biggest loser of them all!"

Everyone was too depressed or drunk to really argue so we all just sort of sat there with equally stupid looks on our faces. Our faces were pretty used to these looks. Over years of practice, our faces had grown accustomed to a vast array of looks that range from apathy, to confusion to stupidity. At this moment, stupidity seemed to be the look of choice.

Finally, Spam O'Mally coaxed his face into forming a somewhat quizzical look, but since his face was so at home looking stupid, quizzical was a bit of an effort. It finally came out looking like a cross between insipidness and paranoia. An entertaining combination, at any rate. After he initiated the expression he finally piped up.

"You mean, a contest?"

"Exactly!" Beamed Dweeb.

"What kind of contest?" Posed Lefty Gristle, who, since he hadn't been drinking as much as the rest of us, had a somewhat easier time shifting his expression to one of puzzlement.

"He who scores with the ugliest girl wins!"

"Wins what?" We all asked in unison. Greed has an amazing way of cutting through any alcohol induced haze.

We all watched with admiration as Dweeb managed to meander through at least four different expressions without once breaking stride. He first struck a firm look of bemusement, before drifting though indifference, making a quick stop at anxiety, and finally rushing headlong into capriciousness. But since none of us knew what capriciousness meant we didn't understand the expression. So Dweeb quickly altered it to a look of audacity, tinged with smugness. The smugness part we recognized, because that's how Dweeb normally looks.

"Losers buy the winner's beers for the next month."

"Great!" Shouted Spanky Peznick. "Hopefully Spam will win. Since he never buys beers anyway we won't notice any difference."

"But how will we determine who's got the ugliest girl?" Chimed in Spam, after he'd administered a firm dig to Spanky's ribs.

"Simple," explained Dweeb, "we vote."

We all nodded our agreement and proceeded to fan out across the lounge.

The first to strike oil was Spam. He'd managed to weasel his way into a conversation with a pair of sisters that looked like they'd flunked out of the Tammy Faye Baker Make-up Academy.

Dweeb wasn't doing too bad either. He'd set up camp at the elbow of some disco queen who hadn't bothered to update her wardrobe since 1978. My guess was that Dweeb took the approach of commenting on how hard it was to find flare leg jeans anymore. I'm sure he also had something to say about the gold-lamme tube-top and her really bitchin' puka-shells and mood-ring.

I saw Lefty making overtures to a woman at the bar who had a look that practically radiated "*bowling alley.*" And Spanky got cornered by a girl who seemed to be trying to coerce him into an arm-wrestling match. My money was on the girl.

I, however, was still sporting the big goose-egg. Nothing seemed to be jumping out at me. . .until I saw "*her.*" And I use the term "*her*" loosely. She was easily no more than four-foot-eleven. And I would be generous if I guessed that she tipped the scales somewhere in the neighborhood of two bucks and some change. She was about as height/weight proportional as a block of granite. It seems she hadn't shaved that morning either. She might as well have hung a sign around her neck saying, "*Win a months free beer here!*"

I sauntered over, as well as one *can* saunter after five pints, and tried striking up conversation.

"Hi!" I garbled. Which is no small task, considering garbling usually needs at least two syllables to garble.

"Hi, yourself." She answered primly.

After completing a full optical tour-of-duty of my person she offered me the seat next to her.

"And what's your name?" She asked smartly.

"Bryan." I answered with what I considered remarkable clarity.

"So, does Bryan like to dance?"

"Yes, Bryan does."

Less than half an instant later I found myself being dragged out onto the dance-floor with a speed that belied her size. Wouldn't you know it, it was a slow song too. It was at this point that a pesky question that had been prancing around in the back or my head, not sitting still long enough to be recognized, finally stepped forward: Just what exactly constitutes "*scoring*?"

While trapped in her vice-like clutches, I glanced around the floor only to see the rest of the guys, equally latched onto, pondering the same question. There was no mistaking the looks we all shared. It was *"meet in the boy's room,"* and we all scampered away at first opportunity.

In the bathroom all eyes turned to me. Dweeb was the first to speak. "I don't know about you guys, but if you ask me, Johnston's got it hands down."

"No question here." Agreed Spam. The rest murmured their agreement.

"Great!" I said. "Then who's buying me my first beer?"

"Hold on, pal! Not so fast. The bet was, he who *scores* with the ugliest girl wins the contest."

A chorus of "yeas," "damn straights," and "you betchas," poured from the guys. This was not a group who easily gave up free beer.

"Wait a minute! If you think I'm gonna sleep with "her" then you've got another think coming! No way, no how! I may be a member of the NO PRIDE CLUB, but there are limits!" I yelled in my defense.

"He does have a point." Agreed Dweeb. "How bout we qualify it as you only have to kiss her?"

"*Hmmmmmmmmm.*" I thought. "*Only kiss her. How bad could that be? Hmmmmmmmmmm.*" I continued thinking. "A *whole month's beer. That could wash any taste out of a guy's mouth. Hmmmmmmmmmmmmmm.*"

"All right, as an official member of the NO PRIDE CLUB, I'll put my best foot forward." The guys all patted me on the back and wished me best of luck, even though I knew they were lying through their teeth.

Moments later I was back, weaving my way through the Shangri-lounge, in search of my prey. It only took a moment before I bumped into her. She seemed pretty happy to see me and even helped me back to my feet again.

"You boys have a nice chat?"

"Swell." I squeaked. I wondered if she could sense my fear as the first beads of sweat began forming on my brow.

"Can I get you a drink?" I offered, looking for anything to shore up my defenses.

"A gin fizz would be marvy!"

"Gin fizz it izz!" I cleverly quipped and hustled over to the bar. Upon arrival, two of the guys came up along side for some general pestering.

"You're a better man than me, Johnston." Offered Spam.

"Better you than me." Added Lefty.

I did my best to ignore them and frantically waved the bartender over. "What drink would you suggest to completely block my senses and alter all my perceptions of reality?"

The bartender pondered that for a moment before snapping his fingers. "Novocain."

"Great. What's in it?"

"Can't say. Most of the ingredients aren't legal in this state."

"I like it already. Pour me one Novocain, straight up."

"One Novocain coming right up. But first I'll need you to sign this waiver releasing me from any legal responsibilities."

I quickly signed the form and waited for my drink. The bartender slipped covertly into the backroom and a moment later brought fourth the elixir. It looked all the world like Windex, and smelled like something I vaguely remember in seventh grade science class. The type of smell you can only get from extreme combustion.

I closed my eyes and tossed back the drink as quickly as I could. I could only taste the cool liquid for about the first eighth of a second. After that my taste buds closed up shop for the night. What shut down next was my peripheral vision, as I began feeling like I was looking down a long dark tunnel. I also discovered a strange sensation in my hands, which had miraculously taken on the sensitivity of oven mitts. Finally, my hearing ability abruptly fell off the scale. After making sure that none of my important organs had been switched off, I turned to make my way back to the table. I'm pretty sure I walked over there, but couldn't really tell, considering that I wasn't terribly sure that I existed below the neck.

After what felt like an eternity, but was probably closer to four seconds, I plopped myself back down at the table and slid the gin fizz over to the girl.

"You OK? You have kind of a blank look on your face." Is what she apparently said. I could see her mouth moving but nothing seemed to be coming out. Somehow, an actual cognitive thought seeped into my

Novocain-enriched brain. To be precise, it was actually a mental-metaphor: I imagined myself standing on the coast, dipping my toe into the freezing water. I knew that slowing easing into the ocean would be a tortuous experience and that simply diving in was always the best thing to do. It's painful for a moment but it's over much faster. It must have been this thought that instigated my next actions. That and the image of free beer for a month.

In one fell swoop I reached across the table, grabbed the girl by the collar and planted a quick dry peck on her lips. Apparently I still had enough common sense in me to make the attempt "*quick*" and "*dry*." But again, with a speed I would have never considered possible for a woman of her density, she grabbed me by the back of the head and quickly turned "*quick and dry*" into "*long and wet*." With some kind of inhuman strength, her tongue pried open my mouth, at which point I felt like my lower organs were being sucked up through my lungs. Visions of countless low-budget horror movies zipped through my head as it occurred to me that perhaps she was inserting an alien-embryo into my stomach. I struggled briefly but came to the quick realization that my efforts were about as effective as throwing marshmallows at a buffalo. I bravely accepted my fate.

The next thing I knew was that she was pulling away and tossing me back, rather unceremoniously, into my chair.

"Thanks pal. Nice knowing you." She then got up from the table and plowed her way through the crowd to a circle of girls that were sitting at the far end of the bar.

The Novocain must have been wearing off a little because I was beginning to discern shapes and sounds again. I could swear I saw her high fiving her friends and saying something to the effect of her never having to buy another beer for the rest of the month. The rest of their conversation I only picked up in small snippets. The terms that seemed to register were, "Whatta geek," "You win," "Was it worth it?" etc.

Hmmm. I thought women weren't allowed in the NO PRIDE CLUB.

20
Road Trip

A car and a tankful of gas; a general destination; no time frame; no map; hardly any food and not nearly enough money. These are the elements of a guy's road trip. A voyage into the unknown that will leave memories in it's path and bruises on our bodies. A trip destined to live forever in our memories but took maybe thirty seconds to plan. In fact, the planning probably took place the night before and was about as in depth as. . .

"Hey, whatyasay we take a road trip?"

"Sure. Where?"

"I dunno. I think my brother's wife's family has a cabin on the coast. Maybe no one's using it this weekend."

"Cool. When you wanna go?"

"First thing in the morning."

"Twelve noon it is."

The groundwork has now been laid for an outing that will surely result in excitement, misery, starvation, sleep deprivation and a boundless supply of story material to be shared over beers. Actually, that's the reason guys take road trips, so that they have new material to entertain each other with.

"So what's new?"

"Nothing."

(Silence)

"Any new scars we ain't seen yet?"

"Nope."

(Silence. Sip.)

"Cops ain't looking for ya for any reason, is they?"

"Nope."

(Sip. Sip. Silence)

"Story-tellin' stockpile sounds like it's gettin kinda low."

"Sure do."

(Sip. Belch. Chuckle. Silence.)

"Reckon we need a road trip."

"Reckon so."

A road trip with the guys is always a lot of fun, but they do have a tendency to take a good six months off your life. That's why women live longer than guys; we take more road trips. You'll notice that life spans were much shorter back in the Middle Ages. That's because everyone was always moving from one place to another, trying to keep a step ahead of whatever plague or disease happened to be in fashion at the time. Life back then was like one big road trip. You either sat in one place and died a particularly nasty death or hit the road with a few cold ones and shaved a few years off that way. Death by road trip was the more preferable of the two.

Can you imagine how old we would grow to if we didn't take so many road trips? Guys would be hitting their sexual peak at thirty five instead of eighteen, we'd be rushing off to buy sports cars for our mid-life crisis at sixty instead of fourty and we'd finally retire at the ripe old age of eighty three. Of course, without road trips adding a little spice here and there we'd probably never reach eighty three because we'd die of boredom.

As with most things in life, the road trips themselves aren't as good as the pre-game hype. Sure, they're a good time, but the way we usually talk about them in advance you'd think we were gonna have a weekend of such decadence and debauchery that if bookies were laying odds on which commandments weren't gonna be broken only, "*Thou shalt not kill*," would be considered a long shot. . .and at seven-to-one at that.

Women take their share of road trips but not nearly as many as guys. It's just something guys do. We can't help it, we're nomadic by nature. Maybe it ties-in with our fear of commitment; our fear of staying with one person, staying in one place for too long. Whatever the reason, we're known for rolling up a few miles on the odometer.

What does one do on road trips? One of the favorite pastimes of course is "*working the skirt*" (i.e: the pursuit of women). You'll notice I said, "*pursuit of*" instead of, "*scoring with*." "*Scoring with*" leads one to assume we actually had success, but, "*scoring with*" is usually a phrase we use before the trip, but doesn't materialize as often as we envision. Like I said earlier, the show doesn't live up to the pre-game hype. It's like the Super Bowl.

The broadcasters talk up the AFC's sacrificial lamb on Super Bowl Sunday knowing full well they're gonna get creamed. They talk about how it could be a high scoring contest, but everyone knows better. Same thing goes for guys before road-trips.

At the start of one road trip a buddy of mine was particularly fired up and went on about how many babes he was gonna nail. He even went out and bought a dozen condoms for the trip.

"Wooo-wee! This is gonna be one hot trip! Babes everywhere! Action galore! And I'll be the out-of-towner so the chicks will have nothing to lose and no worries about me calling back! Wooo-wee!"

Of course, by the end of the trip he was packing away a dozen condoms.

"Stupid chicks. They don't know what they were missing. Their loss. It's not like I was really trying that hard anyway. Stupid chicks. Who needs em? Not me."

The boys have been getting together for weekend road trips since we were old enough to drive; sort of like field trips for a club. But the size of the club always seems to shrink each year for various reasons. On one occasion one of the poor saps knocked-up his girlfriend and wasn't able to join an excursion because he was spending the weekend facing the business end of a shotgun while placing a ring on his sweetie's finger. Another time, one of the guys actually fell in love and got married by choice!

As you're dragged, kicking and screaming toward your thirties, the club's membership innevitably goes down, but occasionally you'll get a new member on leave of absence, or possibly one who pissed off his wife and needs a break from his three-week stint of sleeping on the couch.

It's pretty easy to be a member of the club, you just have to be a guy. It's pretty much the same as the club you were in when you were wearing short pants and playing with army men. The sign on the tree-fort said "no girls allowed," and the same applies for the weekend road trips. I know that what I'm describing applies equally well for women too, so any women reading this, please just insert "*boys*" whenever it says "*girls*," and vice versa.

Even though women go on occasional road trips, too, they've never truly grasped the concept of planning a successful road trip. Basically because they actually *plan* it. They talk about it weeks in advance, stock up on supplies that may be necessary, bring useful things like can openers, and have contingency plans. Someone please explain to me where the hell the fun is in that?

A guy's idea of a contingency plan is having a bottle of Scotch stashed under the front seat in case he runs out of beer. And don't insult our intelligence by even mentioning the possibility of bringing a map along. Getting lost is part of the charm of a road trip–in fact, it's encouraged! One time while backtracking our way through a logging road we were sure would take us to the other side of the Washington Cascade range, my childhood buddy Lefty Gristle had the bad form to pull a map out of the glove compartment. The rest of us exchanged disapproving glances but decided to humor Lefty and take a token glance so as not to hurt his feelings.

To his credit the map was sufficiently torn, dog-eared and weathered so as to be only readable from a distance of two inches in direct sunlight.

"So, where are we?" our disgruntled driver, Spanky Peznick, asked.

"I dunno. Is there any direct sunlight I can hold the map in?"

Being that it was somewhere near the hour of three in the morning, direct sunlight was hard to find in that time zone.

"Is that a good map?" I asked. It must have been the glow from the Zippo lighter Lefty was holding up, because I could have sworn it looked like parchment.

"Of course it's a good map. If it was good enough for my great-grandpappy it's sure as hell good enough for us."

"Ok, fine. So where are we?"

"I dunno. According to the mapmakers, some guys named Lewif and Clart, or something like that, if we follow this trail we'll eventually hit the Pacific Ocean. Hmm that's funny. I didn't know that they still called this part of the country the Oregon Territory."

There was one excursion that painted a vivid picture as to the vast differences between guy's road trips and women's road trips. My friends had gotten wind that some of our female compatriots were taking a holiday on the coast, so at the last minute we decided to do the same. The girls didn't seem to be too thrilled with our decision but figured we'd probably supply high entertainment by doing something stupid. It's good to know our reputation preceded us.

On the day before lift off I swung by the girl's launch pad to see how things were going. I felt like I'd walked into a bee hive. Everyone was in perpetual motion. They milled about checking and double checking to make sure they hadn't forgotten anything. One girl lorded over the room, her eyes darting between her checklist and the roomful of stuff. I stifled a laugh at the neatly organized accoutrements, the matching suitcases, the boxes of food.

"What's with all the stuff?" I asked to the checklist queen.

"Better to have too much than not enough," she said without taking her eyes off the paper.

I walked among the piles, giggling at what they found to be imperative. "*Flashlight? What's up with this?*" I would have educated them on proper road trip etiquette but felt my pearls of wisdom would have fallen on deaf ears. For those of you who don't know already, flashlights are completely optional, especially if you've already got a pack of matches. And if you do have the poor taste to bring one make sure you leave the batteries on the kitchen counter. Of course, if you do bring batteries they should always be the wrong size.

"What's this thing?" I asked, picking up this soft foamy pad.

"Bed roll." she mumbled.

"*Bed roll?*" I puzzled, "*What are they thinking?*" It started to look like they were actually trying to make sure they were comfortable on this road trip. I was beginning to get concerned.

After telling the girls that I'd be over the next morning to help them load the car I left to tell my buddies of the travesty I had just witnessed. We all had a good laugh.

The next day at the crack of noon I dragged myself out of bed and went over to fulfill my obligation. To my dismay I found a note on the door saying that when I hadn't shown up by 7 a.m. they packed up and left.

Upon returning to my house I rallied the rest of the boys out of bed and began preparations.

"How much beer can we fit in the cooler?"

"Oh man, we trashed the cooler at the last bash. Maybe we can just fill up the trunk with ice and throw the beer there."

"If the trunk's filled with beer where will we stow our sleeping bags?"

After weighing the alternatives we decided sleeping bags weren't that important. We grabbed a few bags of chips, a pack of matches, and our sunglasses. All was in ready. After all, it was only a three-day trip.

Ten minutes out of town we'd accomplished our first mission and managed to get thoroughly lost. Treb Weevil suggested that if we make a left turn at the next four intersections he swore he'd have us back on a familiar road. He was right. We'd managed to make a complete circle and were back to where we began being lost.

Have you ever heard of the million-monkey theory? It's said that if you put a million monkeys in front of a million typewriters, odds are that one of them will happen to hit the right keys to type Tolstoy's *"War and Peace."* It's kind of the same theory with guys being lost. Drive down enough roads and eventually they'll find their way out. This is why guys don't have a time frame when going on road trips.

"When y'all leaving for the coast?"

"It's Sunday, ain't it? Some time today."

"Lessee, it's about fifty miles. When d'you expect to get there?"

"Dunno. I reckon before sunset. . .on Tuesday or Wednesday."

"Yeah. If traffic's good."

The million-monkey theory panned out and before it got dark we were back on the highway. We'd polished off the chips and had the alarming revelation that the heat from the muffler right under the trunk was melting our beer ice. We doubled our drinking efforts and succeeded in finishing off most of our cache before the cans got too hot to pick up. Three-Fingered Swede still made an effort and very nearly became Two-Fingered Swede when a smouldering beer can cauterized his hand. I've got a hunch police are gonna have a heck of a time getting fingerprints from him ever again.

By midnight we'd succeeded in losing ourselves a respectable three more times. We would have only gotten lost twice more but Dweeb did some quick thinking and offered up a short cut that took us to some backwater town where everyone seemed to be related. When the townsfolk began gathering on the village green carrying torches we took that as our sign to hit the bricks. We swallowed our pride long enough to ask a bald-headed kid playing a one-sided version of dueling banjos for directions and eventually found our way to a paved road.

By 3 a.m., the gas tank was taking on a decidedly hollow sound so we decided to stop for the night in a deserted parking lot. Trying to sleep four guys in a '81 Dodge Diplomat is no small task but we carried it off without a hitch--unless of course you expect anyone to do any real sleeping. We managed to do a lot of griping and cursing but sleep was pretty much catch as catch can.

When the sun began filtering its way through our grime-encrusted windshield we agreed to take another stab at finding the coast. Since we had the good taste to not have a map, and weren't about to ask some idiot grease monkey for directions, we used the next best thing for finding our way around; we looked out the window.

"Hey, isn't that the girls' cabin about three blocks down the street?"

Our innate sense of direction had come through, again.

Of course, in the three blocks from the parking lot to the girls' cabin we succeeded in getting lost once more before rolling up to the front door. It never ceases to amaze me how Dweeb knows about all these short cuts.

When the first smell of bacon drifted by us we practically crushed each other in a stampede for the kitchen. The girls were sitting around the table, sipping cappuccino and dining on flapjacks, bacon and cantaloupe. We stood there, drooling, looking like a band of escaped convicts who'd broken out by tunneling through two miles of clay.

"There you are," chirped one of the annoyingly perky, well-rested girls. "Anyone interested in breakfast? Clean up your drool and have a seat."

The idea of flapjacks and bacon on a road trip was well beneath our dignity but out of respect for their feelings we reluctantly accepted.

After I managed to Indian-wrestle the last crumbs of toast from Dweeb we settled down long enough to thank the girls for their hospitality. We were sorely tempted to chastise them for their lack of road-trip savvy but I felt that was a lecture best left until after my fourth cappuccino.

21
Where's the Weirdest Place You Did It?

While you and your buddies are out tipping a few adult beverages, there's an extremely good chance that sometime during the evening the topic of conversation will be sex. Not enough, who with, last time, etc. If everyone is in a saucy mood and the personality toggle switch is in the "*on*" position, the sex topic will get even more narrowed down to everyone's favorite sex question: "*Where's the weirdest place you've done it?*"

If you know your friends even marginally well you'll know this information and could probably give them all nicknames categorizing each one.

"Oh, here comes Mister 'On the hood of the Dodge Dart,' or, "Well, if it isn't Miss 'On my parents solo-flex machine.'"

Whenever someone tells one of his friends of the time he had sex in a really strange location one question that no one ever bothers to ask is "*Why*?" Why did he have sex hanging from a tree branch? Why did he have sex on the stove? It's obvious. The reason no one asks is because everyone already knows the answer: You have sex in really strange places so you can tell someone later when the question is asked.

I think women are more into it than guys. Guys won't single out a strange place to do it, they just *want* a place to do it. Women will see an opportunity for sex in a goofy location and make the play.

A guy and his girlfriend could be at a children's park on the swing when the girl suddenly has this brilliant idea. "Honey? Have you ever done it on a swing before?"

"Uh. Ahem. No. . .have you?"

"Nuh-uh. Wanna?"

"Ah. Um. Sure. . .how?"

"Here. You sit down. Then I'll climb on."

"Will we swing when we're doing it or just sit here?"

"Don't be silly. Now hold still."

"Ouch. Careful. This is tricky."

"Hold still, I need to hold on to the chains for balance. Whoops! Heh-heh."

"Ow, the rubber seat is digging into my hip! Oops! Uh. Hold it, hold it. . .there. How's that feel?"

"I dunno, the chain's chaffing against my leg. Oof. Ow. Oh wait. Wait, that's better. Here I'll try to get us to swing now. Hold on. Here, shift your weight. C'mon, you're not shifting."

"Ow! Careful!! Ow! Ow! Ow! That's me you're shifting!"

"Sorry. Here, lean back. Wait not that far! No! Stop!"

After you've stopped rolling around in pain and picked yourself off the dirt, you chalk it up to yet another weird place you can say you did it. Of course, nobody ever asks how good it was in any of these weird places so it doesn't matter that it only lasted a grand total of thirteen seconds and left you with enough abrasions to look like you were attacked by a gang of thugs wielding sand paper.

My friend Schlep Weeblow once told me of a situation he was in that bears repeating. You see, while on vacation in Hawaii Schlep had the pleasure of meeting a fabulous New Zealand babe who took an immediate interest in the Schlepster. According to Schlep he was careful not to work too fast for fear of chasing her off–that and the annoying fact that she was married to some New Zealand soccer god. Of course, the soccer god wasn't on the trip with her, and apparently she wasn't too happy with the marriage, what with her hubby's propensity for practicing his slide-tackles on her. But I digress. Schlep liked having this gorgeous babe hanging around him and didn't want to blow it. As per usual, what did this brand of nice-guy thinking get him? Bupkus. Nada. Nothing. She may have been married but she had a secret agenda Schlep wasn't aware of yet. He soon found out what that agenda was.

Poor Schlep, still playing the nice guy, offered to take his lovely young side-kick to the airport for her trip back to Kiwiland. The flight was delayed an hour so what does Miss "*I'm unhappily married*" do? She grabs Schlep and plants a big ol' wet one on him; a big fat lip lock, complete with a side order of tongue. Needless to say, The Schlepster was a bit stunned. But he was unprepared for what came next.

"Let's find a place to make love!" she cooed.

With the speaking of these words, time came to an abrupt halt. It's moments like this that you think, "This is gonna make the best drinking story ever told!" Schlep got so excited his brain completely vapor-locked. It was like all thirty-seven billion brain cells went on lunch break at once. If someone had tapped him on the side of the head they would have heard a low, hollow, ringing sound.

He stood there for a good few seconds, his jaw hanging somewhere around his waist, his eyes gleaming with a very taxidermy-esque glaze, and his breath stopped altogether. The eventual lack of oxygen finally kick-started his body into action.

"Oh really?" He cleverly quipped.

At this point he broke into a dead sprint, dragging his nymphet in tow.

"Where can you have sex in an airport?" half his brain shrieked at him. "Haven't you mapped out potential places for every contingency?" bellowed the other half.

At this point he told himself that the moment he got home he'd sit down and determine where the most opportune sexual locations would be in every public building he could come up with. You see, had he been female he would have already done this long ago. So he did the next best thing: he asked the girl. She listed off a good dozen or so suggestions ranging from elevators to deserted baggage X-ray tables.

Schlep frantically searched for elevators, vacant restrooms, storage closets, anything that had at least one cubic foot of space and didn't have any more than two people already there. No dice. He tore and wrenched at chained doors, fully expecting his hormone, and adrenaline-soaked system to rip the steel to shreds. But his all-too-human body betrayed him. Finally he collapsed, exhausted, against a vending machine, with much cursing and gnashing of teeth.

Time was up. The babe boarded the plane, Schlep got no action, and would have no drinking story to tell.

Had he pulled that little escapade off, other than having a great drinking story, he would have been a definite crowd pleaser in the next round of "I never." "I never" is an entertaining little game you play, almost exclusively with mixed company after you've had too many drinks of an alcoholic nature. In case you've never played, the group of you sit around and the first person says something that they've never done. If anyone has ever done that then they have to drink. I can assure you that 99% of the "I nevers" are sexually related. Be warned: If you plan on playing don't expect to ever pursue a political career.

I can just imagine everyone's surprise if someone tossed out an obscure little "I never," like, "I've never had sex in an airport." At which point, chances are, everyone would be tipping back their beer. . .except Schlep. Everyone would then gaze at him with undisguised admiration.

"You had sex in an airport?"

"Yep."

"Where'd you do it?"

"Lost luggage room."

Schlep would have then spent the rest of the evening basking in this glory. So, the next time your girlfriend wants to have sex in some really goof-ball place, like your neighbor's tree fort, or a flight simulator, you can rest assured she only wants to do it so she's got her bases covered for the next game of "*I never.*"

22
In Search of the Dirty Girl

Webster's dictionary tells us that the word "*hunger*" means *a craving or urgent need for food or a specific nutrient. A weakened condition brought about by prolonged lack of food. A strong desire.* (For the purposes of this chapter, any words alluding to food can be presumed to also be alluding to sex.)

Sexual starvation is something all men go through, whether it's from bad luck, the planets not being in line, or maybe just a silly haircut. However it happens, it just does--and it sucks.

Since the beginning of time, man's primal instincts have told us to find some action of the carnal variety. Heck, any man feels that a little action is better than no action. Because, after weeks, possibly months, or (God forbid) years of banishment from the female community, any crumb of passion is a meal.

So, how do you end the hunger pangs? Simple. Every guy knows the easiest way to put some food on the table is by finding "the dirty girl."

Let's think about what goes through the mind of a man during a slump. There are feelings of hopelessness, despair, pain, ugliness, etc. The list could go on forever. There's a new crappy feeling for every time you face rejection. One thing, however, drives a man crazier than anything in the world; it's seeing the beautiful knockout with the total dropout.

If you're in a slump and see some yo-yo with the woman of your dreams it can lead you to the brink. You get to that point when Satan himself starts whispering in your ear; telling you all about the nights that dogface has been with the dreamboat. At this point, there is only one answer. . .take it down a notch; forget about the beautiful woman, it's time to find the dirty girl.

When it comes to sex, the mentality of man is primeval and extremely basic. It's best summed up in one classic quote: "*The worst sex I ever had was outstanding!*"

Like any other women, dirty girls come in all shapes, sizes and personalities. But there's one constant; with the dirty girl. . .every guy's got a shot! Even the guy in the slump.

Let me use yet another sports analogy to illustrate. Have you ever watched kids go bumper bowling? It's a great way to build their confidence and get them interested in the game. You see, the lanes are lined with padded bumpers, so you can't throw gutter balls. The ball just bounces off on it's merry way toward the pins.

That's basically what it's like when a guy makes a play on the dirty girl. Your approach and delivery can stink, but unless you're a flailing madman it's damn near impossible to come off without scoring a couple of points.

Of course, scoring a strike with the dirty girl isn't necessarily a lock. Why? Because there are plenty of other guys around who are in the same predicament as you; hungry, starved, horny.

You see, the dirty girl has major sex appeal. What is that appeal? Simple. Most guys think they have a chance at having sex with the dirty girl and that sounds appealing. But there's something more to the dirty girl, something different. Is it her ability to go head-to-head with you on tequila slammers. . .and *then* cap the night with a shot of rot-gut Canadian whiskey? Is it the black stockings, short skirt and low-cut blouse? Is it the tattoo of the snake that's wrapped around her ankle, that makes her special? Maybe it's her pointy-toed boots or five-inch stiletto heels? Maybe it's her tendency to throw out timely expletives? In addition to her talk it might be her walk? Maybe the way she dances?

The answers? Yes, yes, yes, yes and yes.

There are a ton of different types of dirty girls, and the sight of one is all it takes to bring back a guy's shattered confidence. He knows he's got a shot, and that's all a guy needs right there--hope. It's a fact that more times than not, the starving man will still fail to find quality nourishment, but he still has that image of hope!

Picture, if you will, a refrigerator door. There may be nothing inside, but with the door closed you can't tell. It could be filled with all sorts of delicacies. There's a chance the hunger could be appeased. One meal can't last a lifetime, but it can sure buy some sanity; and when it gets to a point where your evening fantasies involve visualizing the last time you and Mister Happy had a date with Rosie Palm, you know it's time to stoop. . .to the dirty girl.

There have been more than a few occasions when I've been in search of the dirty girl. Many times it was because my buddy Nob had just come into town. Nob, like most men, is a member of the fabled NO PRIDE CLUB, and always calls me because he knows I'll be up for the quest.

Nob is the perfect buddy in a time of drought. He brings back the spirit. He knows that a slump can be an enjoyable time because it involves the chase--getting back in the game. Failure is common. Failure is okay. But failure to try is unacceptable; it's just plain chicken. And no man wants to be called poultry.

The veteran in the dirty girl game doesn't waste any time going to a nice pub that serves micro-brews in the university community. Nope. Too young. Too much work. And maybe too much competition from well-groomed college studs who can actually bench press four times their IQ. No, you've got to find a place that's a little dark and has a cheesy two-man band playing lousy cover tunes on their 1978 simulated wood-sided synthesizer in the corner. And smoking is required. If you don't smoke, it won't matter because you'll be inhaling about the equivalent of seventy eight cigarettes over the course of an hour anyway.

Finding a seat close to the dance floor is a bonus. Get a table, make sure there are extra chairs, and don't let someone from another table take your chairs from you! They may look like cheap chrome and vinyl but in reality they're gold. Guard them with your life. Eventually, if it's a relatively crowded place, those seats will be in high demand. With spare seats you now have bargaining chips. When you spot the dirty girl standing in the corner, sucking the life out of a gin and tonic, as her knees begin to wobble. . .you act.

If she truly is a dirty girl she'll have no problem with your invitation. However if she's a dirty girl wannabe you may be forced to throw her one of your time-honored and well-oiled pick-up lines, such as. . .

"Excuse me, do you have a quarter? My mom always told me that I had to call her when I met the woman of my dreams." If she's still playing hardball you can soften her up with this smile-getter. . .*"Can I buy you a drink or do you just want the cash?"* If she walks away from that one, forget her, she's not worth the effort—not dirty enough.

Like I said before, occasional failure is a given but at least you've laid some foundation. After another hour of standing and a couple of highballs it might be she who comes crawling back, begging for a place to sit.

I can recall numerous dirty girl excursions with good ol' Nob. On one occasion I knew we were in for some high entertainment. Why? Because Nob told me how things had been pretty slow back at his residence in Whoville, USA. How slow? So slow he was considering parking his convertible across the street from the local high school, waiting for the bell to ring, looking for a sixteen year old tart who's tired of playing with *"boys."* Needless to say, Nob was glad to be back in the big city.

On this evening, we decided to go to our favorite house of filth. We'll just call it *"Tank's swill joint."* Of course, it was Thursday Night: (dirty) ladies night, as we like to call it. Women get any drink for maybe fifty cents off and, well, us guys get to sit back and watch a gaggle of gals bludgeon each other at the bar in an attempt to take advantage of the cheap hooch.

Like every Thursday night at "*Tank's*," the band was lousy. But that's all right because the dirty girl often has bad taste in music. We were lucky that evening, it only took one quick glance around the bar to decide which dirty pair to pursue: the ones with the glossy eyes and big boobs.

With a few well-placed comments about the bitchin' monster truck race coming to town and the virtues of heavy metal we managed to coax our prey over to our table. The two girls were named Kiki and Deb. As for Kiki, I figured it was a safe bet her name was usually seen in red neon outside "*The Golden Girl Massage Parlor*" on First Avenue. And after listening to Deb speak I couldn't help but wonder if Deb was short for "debilitated." What a voice! So deep, worn and scratchy; kind of like what mineworkers with a good case of blacklung must sound like after a long night of hard drinking, only to wake up and chug a glass of sand and finely ground fiberglass. But it's funny how that miracle bra she was sporting made her voice sound like the song of a nightingale.

Nob isn't one for dancing, but the veteran that he was, knew it would be required if he was going to get the bat off his shoulder. When the girls resisted our first swoops we knew there was no time to waste. It was time for "*body shots*."

The "*body shot*" is a fail-safe method for instigating naughty behavior. I casually mentioned a great new drinking game I'd heard about and promptly got the girl's attention. Dirty girls love drinking games.

"How do you play?" asked Kiki.

"It's really simple," I cooed. "All you need is some salt, a lime wedge, a shot of tequila and a neck."

"Ooooh. Sounds cool," growled Deb. "Show me first!"

It didn't take too much arm twisting for me to cave in to her demands.

"Ok, show me your neck," I demanded. Deb then gigglingly tipped her head back. "I have to sprinkle salt on your neck, but for the salt to stick, first it's got to be wet." At this point I then proceeded to lick her neck with a great deal of enthusiasm. I then followed up by sprinkling a healthy dash of salt on the desired area.

"Place the lime wedge in your mouth," I explained, and promptly went to work sucking the salt off her exposed flesh. By the time that I'd finished with that, I noticed Deb's eyes had mysteriously rolled back into the farthest reaches of her skull and that she was doing a remarkable job of crushing the arm rests of her chair with an impressive display of grip strength. I cast a quick glance at an astonished Nob and Kiki before throwing back the tequila, and soon after made a mad dash for the lime wedge. Taking a wedge of lime from someone's teeth can be a very simple task. Taking it with your own teeth makes it much more exciting. Especially when the other person has pulled the wedge into the back of their mouth and has begun playing a game of hide and seek with the wedge and your tongue.

After several moments with my tongue doggedly trying to corral the lime I managed to secure the pesky citrus and withdrew my prize. Deb had succeeded in ripping out a goodly portion of my hair by this point and was frantically waving for the waitress to bring us another round. By now, Kiki and Nob had taken on a rather glazed, sweaty look--a look usually reserved for people who've just witnessed their first porno movie--and immediately joined in on the frantic waitress wave!

Nob and I knew our mission was accomplished. These two were in the bag. In a matter of hours the drought would be over and the hunger pangs silenced.

Bad bands, cheap perfume, big hair and heavy make-up. It's amazing what you'll put up with in search of. . .a little dirt.

23
People-Watching and Friendly Stalking

People are so transparent. We're always coming up with some pathetic excuse for why we're doing something we're slightly ashamed of. Case in point: people-watching. That's what we say we're doing when actually all we're doing is scoping; checking someone out. When you "*people-watch*," you're looking for only one of two things, freaks and knockouts. Otherwise, what's the point? Normal, everyday people are boring to watch.

"Hey, look at that guy! He looks just like my neighbor! Wow! And look, he's watching that old woman over there who looks like that old woman over there! This is great! Ha-ha! I can't wait to tell everyone about this tomorrow!"

Wheee.

When I'm "*people-watching*," I want that one percent of one percent. I'm looking for the weirdo with the day-glo orange mohawk and eighty percent of his body covered with tattoos of snakes and a skull with "*Mom*" printed under it. If I can't find him to roll my eyes at, then I want to watch gorgeous babes with perfect bone structure and bodies that were carved from countless hours on a Nordic-Trak.

I'm always hearing people say what a great time they had "*people-watching*" at the county fair, or the music festival in the park, or wherever they were slumming over the weekend. What they're really saying is that they saw lots of weirdos whom they'd never consider letting their daughter get within spitting distance of, or that they saw a bevy of beautiful people whom they'd love to get within spitting distance of. (There I go ending a sentence with a preposition, again. *WARNING:* Kids, do not write like me, unless you want to see your grammar-teacher's hair turn grey before your very eyes, and your grades plummet into oblivion.)

Ok, back to our story. Do you really think staring at someone who looks like Joe Average is terribly stimulating? I don't. But we all seem to use that thinly-veiled excuse whenever it's convenient. If you *are* staring at Joe Average or Josephine Average then you're not scoping, you're comparing. You're checking them out to see how they stack up. In other words, you're sizing up the competition.

Have you ever noticed how the way we "*people-watch*," completely changes with the company we keep?

It's true! If you're sitting in a restaurant booth across from your girlfriend you certainly won't be gawking at the curvacious wonder who just entered the room. Not a chance. If you're caught checking out another babe, you'd better be quick at hitting the shield button before you take a steak knife in the esophogus.

Getting caught browsing can be hazardous, so as a public service to our male readers let me offer some pointers on how to ease out of the situation as seamlessly as possible.

Step one: Don't panic. Panic admits guilt, and a guy will never plead guilty to checking out a babe while with his girlfriend.

Step two: Quickly find something wrong with the woman who caught your eye. Even if it's Michelle Pfeiffer who walked through the door. Lie. If you can, throw out a comment about her shoes. Not only will you dumbfound your girlfriend, but she'll appreciate your eye for fashion. It doesn't matter whether or not your girlfriend thinks Michelle's shoes are cute, she'll be impressed that you cared what kind of shoes she was wearing. Of course, you may find yourself having to deal with her pointing out everyone's shoes for the next six months, now that she's become aware of your eye for foot apparel, but at least it got you out of the initial trouble and that's what we're here to take care of. As I've pointed out before, guys don't worry about troubles in the future, it's the here and now that's important.

If you were in the same situation with your buddy Fred, things would be completely different. First of all you'll probably shatter his wrist in an attempt to get him to turn around to. . .uh, check out the remarkable artwork standing, er, hanging by the entrance. If he's got the brains of a walnut he'll be clued-in by your salivating and panting so he knows what he's really being jerked around to look at. And if the *"artwork"* is wearing a mini-skirt he may even forgive you for the fractured ulna you've just inflicted on him.

Instead of two guys hanging out, suppose it's two girls? In the case of women, their first optic sensation will illicit a different response. They'll check out the clothes first. It doesn't matter if it's a man or woman who enters the room, the first thing that gets reviewed is the attire. Of course, they will have a tendency to be a bit more critical of their female counterparts.

For example: Woman with nice body enters the room in form-fitting outfit. _Response_. . .

"Check out the bimbo! Does she have a job or does she just work out all the time? She probably couldn't spell 'cat' if you spotted her the 'C' and the 'A'."

Man with well built physique enters the room in torn jeans and t-shirt. _Response_. . .

"Hmmmmmmmmmmm. Gotta love the basics."

Woman with fair body but wearing an outstanding ensemble from Nordstrom enters the room. _Response_. . .

"Oh, look at what she's wearing! You would look so cute in that. Hey, check out her shoes! Hmmmm. She's probably just dressing like that to make us look bad. What a bitch. I'm sure her daddy paid for the whole thing. Probably never worked a day in her life. She probably sleeps around too. Slut."

Skinny, wormy, accountant-like guy wearing Armani suit stumbles into room. _Response_. . .

"Nice suit."

If just watching isn't stimulating enough you may want to take it to the next step: "*Friendly stalking.*" Now I know the word "*stalking*," immediately conjurs up bad images. Thoughts of Peeping Toms who slink around windows and terrorize you at all hours of the night come to mind. "*Stalking*" is also a word that many equate with National Geographic or the Discovery Channel when they're airing a special on leopards and their prey. But friendly stalking is just what it sounds like, friendly! It's pleasant, harmless and gets the endorphins pumping. It's a good thing!

Friendly stalking includes such ridiculous pastimes as driving past a good-looking girl's house to see if she's home, whose car is in front of her house, or if the light is on in her second floor bedroom window. It gives our imagination something to work with. All right, sure, It's kind of pathetic, but being pathetic is something we've come to accept in the hunt for the ellusive babe.

There are many facets to friendly stalking; no set rules, no right or wrong way. As long as you're caught up in the thrill of the chase then everything's cool. One of my favorite friendly stalks is when you see the good-looking girl coming out of the diner downtown. *Hmmm. Does she eat there regularly? Does she work nearby?* More data is needed, so you stalk. You follow at a safe distance to see where she's going. *Ah ha! She's going into the mall! Does she work there or is she shopping? Oops, there she goes into the Eddie Bauer store. I'll wait.* Ten minutes of trying to look nondescript passes and she still hasn't left. Chances are she works there. Over the next week you've suddenly got this urge to shop at Eddie Bauers--every single day--at the same time every single day. Funny thing is you never buy anything. Of course you never talk to her either because you're too chicken.

You stalked, you got the necessarry information and what did you do with it? Zippo. All stalk, no action.

Probably the most important device involved in friendly stalking is the trusty automobile. You're cruising along when suddenly, off to the right, you see a person with long blonde hair walking with traffic. This woman (or man) knows nothing of your attempts to see how good he (or she) looks, and that, while trying to check them out, you nearly ran over a seventy eight year old man with a walker. You had no intentions of bad deeds, you just wanted a look. Was she young? Was she old? Was she a he? Damn that long hair!

Many times the friendly stalking doesn't have anything to do with looks, it may simply have something to do with the stalkee's availability. That's where the "tour of duty" comes in.   What's the "tour of duty?" Simple. The "tour of duty" (from a guy's perspective) starts with an overall perusal of the individual's body. Focus is then shifted to the chest. After a lengthy rest there the eyes then do a brisk jog up to the face, after which they scamper back down to the chest, halting only briefly to catch their breath before hurrying down to the legs for a couple of laps and then back up for a refresher course on the chest and finally down to the hand--the left one to be specific--the ring finger on that hand to be even more specific.

When he sees Mount Everest sitting on that dainty little appendage the first thoughts that will go through his head will range from,"*Damn!*" to any number of similar terms that in printed text are normally referred to by way of asterisks and ampersands (@#&!).

There is never a time when the "tour of duty" does not reach the ring finger. It's automatic. Women are probably not even aware that men will actually drive an extra seven to nine blocks out of their way, weaving recklessly through traffic, in an effort to catch up with the brunette in the white convertible Cabriolet to see if she's sporting karats on her hand.

After catching up at the next stop light, the man of course will do nothing more than peer over at her because he just wants to know her status, and he's probably too chicken to do anything else. He may have been hoping to receive a wink or possibly an accidental glance in his direction, but the average guy will just go his merry way after that. A glance or a smile from any gal on the road can ease all traffic hassles, because that meant she dug you. Even if it was only for a micro-second, she dug you! (At least, that's what we tell ourselves.) All the weaving through traffic and trying to dodge the kids at the elementary school cross-walk was worth it. Even if you do have to spend twenty minutes trying to pry that little tennis shoe out of your car's grille.

24
The Sucker

Poor Bruce. All he wanted was a little action to cheer him up, and what he got was a roundhouse right to his ego that would have made Mike Tyson proud.

While lamenting our lack of dates, Bruce told me his tale of "*whoa!*". Tales of "*whoa!*" are easily confused with tales of woe because they both usually end up streaked with misery and dabbling in the realm of patheticness. (If there is such a word as patheticness.) The big difference between tales of woe and "*whoa!*" is that tales of woe are generally sad affairs whereas tales of "*whoa!*", while equally sad, are usually pretty funny. The humor, most often, is a direct result of the sadness and misery, and like I've said before, humor is almost always at it's best when it's at the expense of someone else.

Another difference between the types of tales is that tales of *"whoa!"* usually leave you saying, "*Whoa!*", after you hear them.

What happened went something like this. . .

Bruce had been dateless for a while and decided he'd gone celibate long enough. He decided to call his "*sure thing.*" Most people have, at one time or another, had their own, personal, *"sure thing."* They're usually ex-girlfriends, or boyfriends, as the case may be, that you call up when you're really feeling the need. There isn't usually any messy emotional stuff getting in the way either, it's just a mutual understanding between consenting and sexually frustrated adults.

At any rate, Bruce gave his "*sure thing*" a call and she was more than happy to comply! "Just leave it to me, Bruce, I'll plan the perfect evening!"

Bruce was thrilled! This was better than he could have hoped for! He didn't have to do any planning, all he had to do was show up. Beautiful!

When the big night finally arrived Bruce was in high spirits. The streak was about to come to a close and there was much rejoicing. He was beginning to think the expiration date on "*Mr. Contraceptive*" was going to come and go, and that is not a club you want to become a member of.

Condoms have a shelf life of something like six months, which may not sound like that long, but if you're the one who's actually watched the expiration date pass between the times you've had sex then it feels like an eternity. As an act of compassion, contraceptive manufacturers should try to develop condoms that have a half-life of something like plutonium or Twinkies so that no man should be embarrassed that he actually had to throw their product out for lack of use.

One time my buddy Three-Fingered Swede, in a swaggering act of shear ego, went out and bought himself a gross of rubbers. For reasons we never could fathom, he thought he was about to go through some sort of nutso summer of decadence and debauchery. Yea, right. In just another showing of God's unique brand of humor, The Swede came down with some sort of weird skin rash that made him look something like a cross between a radish and a hedgehog. It wasn't terribly attractive, and needless to say, The Swede went dateless for a while. If I remember correctly it was approximately seven months, two weeks and twelve hours before The Swede finally coerced some girl into going out with him. Actually, I'm positive that's how long it was because I'm listening to some music on the CD player I bought with the winnings from the bet my other buddies and I were running. We all coughed up fifty bucks apiece to predict when The Swede would get a date. We each bet on three month windows and I had the six to nine month gap. Of course, to help solidify my chances of winning I made it a point to let The Swede know how scratching a rash lends itself to a speedy recovery, and how lanolin and other such lotions are just a marketing scam and offer no benefits. The Swede, being The Swede that he is, lapped up my ready wisdom and never gave it a second thought for at least the first four months. When he finally went and saw a doctor, half the occupants in the waiting room, upon seeing a large, splotchy, reddish, vaguely human-looking, walking abrasion enter the room, either hurled into the nearest wastepaper baskets or ran screaming for the parking lot. It was about this time that The Swede finally figured that he'd been given poor advice.

But I digress. Bruce was not about to become a member of the condom expiration club and went forth with great purpose. When he finally got to the girl's place he was pretty fired-up and his hormones were getting ready to start billing overtime. "Hi, Missy!"

"Hi, Bruce! Can I get you a drink?"

"No thanks, let's have sex!"

"Aren't you the impatient one. Hold your horses, there's plenty of time for that."

"No. Really, there isn't. My expiration date is midnight tonight."

"I don't know what you're talking about but don't worry, we'll be back before midnight."

The first cracks of suspicion began forming in Bruce's hormone-saturated mind. "What do you mean, 'back before midnight?' Where are we going, and more importantly, why are we going? The only place I want to go is into your bedroom! It's seven o'clock, I've only got five hours left!"

Bruce was obviously confused by this sudden change in protocol. Normally when he and she got together is was always perfectly straightforward and by-the-book. He'd show up, they'd grope, they'd have sex and he'd go home. Textbook. This deviation from the normal game-plan didn't sit very well with him but the "sex" carrot was still dangling in front of him so he grudgingly went along.

"So, where are we going, Miss 'I'll plan the perfect evening'?"

"Well, first I thought we'd meet some friends of mine in the south end for drinks. If that's okay with you?"

"Yea, yea, sure, sure. As long as we're back soon."

Bruce was too focused on the pot of gold to concern himself with why they had to travel forty five minutes to join her friends for drinks.

An excruciating forty five minutes later (at least for Bruce's hormones) they pulled up in front of the Red Lion hotel.

"We're meeting your friends at a Red Lion hotel? What, they know the bartender here and can get free drinks or something?"

Bruce didn't seem to notice her sudden sheepishness. "Yea, heh, heh, something like that."

They strolled into the lobby and she herded Bruce over to the elevator.

"Wait a minute, the lounge is over there!" Bruce pointed out, helpfully.

"We're meeting them upstairs." She mentioned, rather evasively, I might add.

Suddenly it all started to make sense to Bruce. The sly girl *had* planned the perfect evening. She didn't want to have him at home, she went and got them a hotel room for the night! There was probably iced Champaign waiting for them by the king-sized bed and mints on the pillows! This would be well worth the wait.

As she led Bruce out of the elevator she sort of shuffled her feet and mumbled, "I have a confession to make, Bruce, we're not actually meeting my friends for drinks."

"Yea, heh, heh, I just figured that out."

She seemed surprised by this. "You mean you're not angry?"

"Angry? Why would I be angry? This was a great idea!"

This is the part that in literary terms is called, "waiting for the shoe to drop." The shoe was in the form of a conference room with a podium at the head of it bearing a sign that said, "Welcome entrepreneurs!".

It took a few seconds for the whole scenario to fully weave through Bruce's mind. "What the hell is this? We can't have sex here! There's too many people around!"

"No Bruce, I wanted to let you in on a great opportunity that I've been introduced to. It's a sure-fire way to make great money that only takes a small initial investment, and once you've recruited your own team then there's no telling how much money you can make!"

Finally, a small forty watt bulb blinked on inside Bruce's head. "You've brought me to a business recruiting seminar?"

Bruce could hardly believe his eyes. Actually, it wasn't Bruce, as a whole, that didn't believe his eyes, it was more like three or four of his major organs and one extremity in particular that had a hard time grasping the situation. When the harsh reality finally received grudging acceptance by all the body parts Bruce just sort of stood there, looking rather pallid, and feeling a whole lot worse. She'd played him like a cheap violin at the annual sap's convention! She'd thrown out the bait, and he'd gobbled it up without a second look at that sharp, shiny hook that was peeking out. But his self-respect, in it's death spasms, offered one last act of defiance. He was damned if she was gonna reel him in, so he quickly gave her a look that put a permanent kink in her hair and promptly spit out the hook.

Upon hearing this I made sure to give Bruce the proper response.

"Whoa!"

Bruce gave me a look that acknowledged my proper response, and went on with his story.

"To let her know of my displeasure I didn't talk to her throughout the whole two-hour seminar."

"Wait a minute" I said, "You actually stayed for their stupid meeting?"

"Damn right I did!"

"But I thought you spit out the hook! I thought you weren't gonna be her patsy!"

"So I changed my mind, so sue me. I was suffering from ESB (excessive seminal buildup) and saw a cure in sight. I hadn't reached expiration hour yet and wasn't about to let that happen without a fight. I figured that if I waded through the stupid meeting Missy would put out."

"So. . .did she?"

"Damn straight. By eleven-fifteen, I might add. I'm still a proud non-member of the contraceptive expiration club."

"Whoa!" I reiterated. "So what you're saying is that you were so determined to have sex that you actually lowered yourself to be callously taken in by that girl and then sat through the entire meeting, thereby officially labeling yourself a pathetic loser?"

"Hey, I told you it was a tale of 'whoa!'."

I couldn't argue with him there. Next time maybe I'll tell you my own tale of "whoa!". It has to do with a great business opportunity that Bruce has got me involved with.

25
Selective Memory

One fine afternoon my buddy Spam O'Mally and I were reminiscing about our past conquests and failures with women. Not surprisingly, the latter far outweighed the former. As was the custom, we relished the moment over a couple of luke-warm cans of fine malted beverage. Normally we would opt for the slightly less exotic and more economical Schlitz, but the owner of the convenience store, a regular P.T. Barnum incarnate, persuaded us to cut loose and live a little. "*What the hell,*" we figured. "*Let's go for it.*" After long minutes of agonizing over the appropriate brew we finally decided on a six-pack of imports: Pabst Blue Ribbon! Ok, so it's imported from the mid-west, don't kill my buzz! As I was saying, we tucked the beer away as we left the store, knowing full well that if any of our friends spotted us they'd have a field day cracking wise about our *"high-brow"* choice of beer and how it would only be a matter of time before we ditched them for the country-club set. We snuck back to my place and proceeded with our trip down memory lane.

"I tell ya Spam, it feels like only yesterday when me and Babs split up."

"Uh, Bryan. It was yesterday."

"Yea. Then I reckon the feeling's pretty accurate." I swilled the beer around in my can as I got caught up in the moment. "Boy, we sure had some good time, ol' Babs and me."

"Good times?" Spam practically yelled. "You guys fought like Tyson and Holyfield! What good times did you have with her?"

"Ah, Spam, you're just jealous."

"Jealous! She pulled a knife on you?"

"You called that a knife? Besides, it hadn't been sharpened in weeks. Why, I doubt you could hardly dress a decent elk with that blade."

"She was wanted in four states on battery charges!"

"I'd hardly consider Rhode Island a state, Spam. Yep, ol' Babs and I had some special moments."

"Would one of those special moments be when she tried to run you over with your own car?"

"The prosecution never had conclusive evidence that she actually tried to run me over. Her foot just slipped off the brake."

"Bryan, you were up hill from her!"

"Spam, I think you're overreacting."

"Overreacting? You do the same thing with every psycho girl you date. For some unfathomable reason you only remember the good parts, if any, to your relationships. How are you gonna break this nutso pattern if you refuse to accept the, shall we say, unhealthy qualities of past girlfriends? If you don't accept the fact that they're whacked out then you're gonna think all whacked out chicks are normal! Can't you see that?!"

I was beginning to get concerned about Spam. He was really getting wound up, and the foaming at the mouth wasn't exactly helping my appetite.

"Here, Spam, take this napkin and wipe the foam off your mouth. Now settle down. I don't see what you're getting at. Sure, I'd have to say that a few of my past relationships weren't exactly smooth sailing. . ."

"Smooth sailing? The Titanic had smooth sailing compared to your dates!"

"C'mon Spam. I know that Babs had a bit of a temper. . ."

"Temper? If she was any more of a hot-head NASA could pick-up her thermal readings on orbiting satellites."

"All right, all right. So she was a bit quick to judge, at least my other girlfriends were pretty normal."

"Yea, right. Normal. What about Sheila?"

"What about her?"

"Does the *toaster and bathtub incident* ring a bell?"

"You've never wanted to have breakfast in the tub? I thought it was thoughtful and courteous. She probably had no idea that cord would reach that far."

"How about Delilah?"

"Yea?"

"Two words. Ice-pick and waterbed."

I wasn't sure if ice-pick was one or two words but I didn't think Spam was ready to open a dialogue on the subject at that time. "She told me she was trying to kill a fly. The pick was handiest.   She does have excellent hand/eye coordination, you know."

"And then there was Psycho Sally."

"C'mon Spam. You were the only one who referred to her as that."

"That you know of. She was a nut-case, through and through! How many normal people sleep in a bed the shape of a pentagram?"

"Well, I. . ."

"And how many sane persons make it a practice to chant, 'Oh highest Dark One, Prince of the eternal blackness that is my soul, may this food that I am to consume strengthen me to carry out your divine will of world domination,' before sitting down to a meal?"

"Look, did she ever gain world domination? No. So why are you hanging onto that?"

"Then how about what's-her-face, the girl who could never remember your name, even after you guys had been dating for three months?"

Spam went on for several more minutes, reminding me of past relationships that washed up on the rocky shore of good-love-gone-bad. But Spam should have know better than to be throwing rocks in that glass-house he sadly calls a life.

"Okay, Spam, dare I mention a few of your past dalliances?"

"Me? My record's clean. I've yet to date a PBFH (Psycho-Bitch-From-Hell).

"Clean, huh? So I suppose, in your eyes, Carmen the Klepto, was a veritable pillar of virtue."

"Uh. . . . ."

It's not often that Spam is left speechless, but he was busted and he knew it. Spam met Carmen at a swap meet, and if you've ever been to a swap meet then you probably have a good idea of what Carmen looks like. The Lee jeans with the white circle on her back pocket where she kept her tin of Copenhagen handy was the first giveaway. I'm still not completely sure what it was that initially attracted Spam to her but my hunch is that he had been dateless for a spell and was coming up on his contraceptive expiration date and saw Carmen as a cruel gift from the celibacy gods. The celibacy gods are a pretty demanding bunch; not to be taken lightly. They also have a twisted sense of humor. They're not kind, forgiving gods, but one of the old gods. They demand sacrifices pretty regularly, and if they're not pleased with you they can make your sex-life as dry and barren as the Utah salt flats. How they usually work is that they "*grace*" you with their presence for an extended period of time, and then, just to amuse themselves, they'll offer up a particularly nasty looking "*sure thing*" to tempt you. If you take the bait they may actually look upon you with pity and from there on offer you reasonable opportunities at actual relationships. If you ignore the carrot they dangle in front of you they might just decide that you are a godless heathen and make an example of you. And you thought that last dry-spell was just bad luck. Ha! Obviously, at one time or another, you pissed off or ignored a gift from the celibacy gods and were cursed with their extended presence.

At any rate, Spam probably saw Carmen as a token from the celibacy gods and didn't want to look ungrateful. I still remember the moment I first began getting suspicious of Carmen; it was when Spam showed up one day sporting a new watch.

"Hey, Spam, since when can you afford a Rolex? Those babies cost five grand."

"It's a gift from Carmen. Pretty nice, huh?" He gushed, absolutely brimming with naiveté.

"Uh, Spam. You guys have been dating for about two weeks."

"Yea, so?"

"She's chronically unemployed, Spam."

"So, what's your point?" Spam asked, sounding almost realistically wounded. Almost.

"Spam, the woman lives in a double-wide trailer, at the expense of the tax-payer. You do the math."

"Maybe she's been saving up," was all that Spam could muster, all the while shuffling his feet and looking at the floor. Spam knew full-well that she kiped the watch, but he'd always wanted a Rolex, so he let his imagination fill in the gaps. This is gonna sound kind of weird, but the fact that she ripped-off the watch didn't bother me as much as the fact that, here is a woman bold enough and clever enough to score a multi-thousand dollar timepiece but still lives with her mother in a trailer-park, wears AC/DC half-shirts, has hair that's big enough to house small owls and drives a '78, lime-green, TRANS-AM Rally Sport. In other words, she was good enough to be a professional thief but not ambitious enough to pursue it as a viable career. I ask you, what is more disappointing that someone who does not live up to their potential? As it turned out Carmen was more of a *thrill-seeker* crook; strictly small-time. Her trailer was peppered with knick-knacks that she'd absconded with over the years; chia pets, lava-lamps, black-velvet Elvis paintings. It's unfortunate that a woman with her light-fingered gift had such lousy taste.

Her propensity for making off with anything within her grasp didn't seem to bother Spam too much. He just turned a blind eye and hoped that she had the foresight to shoplift something practical, like condoms. Spam enjoyed his little tryst until he started noticing some of his own stuff starting to disappear. At first he didn't seem to mind, since the stuff that was disappearing was junk that he'd just never gotten around to throwing away. Remember, Carmen had really bad taste. If she wanted to score his Welcome Back Kotter action figures, she was welcome to them; besides, he hadn't played with them in months. But everyone has their limits, and as a result the honeymoon soon came to a crashing halt.

Spam has as much tasteless junk as the next person and Carmen was more than welcome to rip it off if she so desired. In fact, Spam was starting to see her as a convenient trash-removal service. But someone should have warned Carmen that there is one object of Spams that is untouchable; an object of such profoundly deep meaning to Spam that none of us is really sure why he's so hung up on it. Sitting proudly in his kitchen, next to the veg-o-matic that he picked up for a song at a garage sale, is Spam's pride and joy: a beer-mug crafted from a reindeer hoof. I can't recall a party where Spam didn't have the hoof-mug firmly in his grasp. It was about a foot tall, and like most reindeer hooves, was covered in short, bristly fur. And since the base of the mug was the hoof itself, with the toes (if that's what you call them) pointing sharply down, you couldn't set the mug down, otherwise it would tip over. That never seemed to cause a problem with Spam since I don't think he's ever set a beer mug down once he's got it in his grasp. No one is really sure where Spam got this thing, and when asked he just shrugs it off indifferently, "Oh, I just picked it up somewhere."

We knew better. I recall one time when some gorilla with a bad attitude and an even worse sense of timing tried to take Spam's hoof-mug from him at a party. By the time the paramedics had successfully pried the gorilla's head out of the heating duct my guess is that he figured it out that the mug was off-limits. For whatever reason, that mug was Spam's Holy Grail. . .as Carmen soon discovered.

I was over at Spam's house playing some video games when I went into the kitchen to grab us a couple of beers. As I turned to leave I had this weird feeling that something wasn't quite right; that something was missing. I'd been in Spam's kitchen a bazillion times and knew it like the back of my hand. In fact, I'd probably been in it more than Spam had, so trust me when I tell you that I could sense something amiss. After a quick scan of the shelves, I saw the vacant space where the hoof-mug normally perched. At first I just figured maybe it was in the dishwasher, but I immediately ruled that out because I don't think Spam's ever figured out how to use it. Actually, I don't think Spam's ever figured out how to use anything that remotely resembles a cleaning device. Show him a broom and he'll just give you a puzzled look; like you just held up some strange artifact freshly dug up on an archaeological expedition in the Sudan.

Upon realizing that the mug wasn't in the dishwasher, the unthinkable passed through my head: Carmen kiped it! The early stages of panic began to coagulate in my brain. If Spam discovered that his little bed-mate had lifted his prize mug there's no telling how ballistic he could go. I immediately opted for preventative measures.

When I went back into the living room I asked Spam if I could use his phone in the bedroom to make a call. He waved me off, too engrossed in trying to take out a demon-warrior with a particularly nasty looking weapon. As soon as I got on the phone I called Three-fingered Swede, Yank Pudweller, Spanky Peznick, and Dweeb Thingus, to tell them what had transpired and to come up with a game-plan for keeping Spam off death row for chopping up Carmen with a dull garden implement. I told them to meet me at Carmen's trailer as soon as possible. There was no telling when Spam would notice the missing mug, and it wouldn't take long for him to come to the same realization as me.

I told Spam I was late for something or other and bolted for the door. Luckily, he was still in the process of decapitating some pesky troll-like vermin and didn't give my departure a second thought.

By the time I'd gotten to Carmen's trailer the rest of the guys were already milling about. There was no disguising their fear.

"Any ideas?" I offered up.

"A couple of National Guard units would be helpful." Pointed out Spanky.

"Actually, I think this may be our only hope." Said The Swede, as he held up small black device that looked all the world like something from a Lost in Space episode.

"Is that a Tazer?" I asked.

"Yep. I touch him with this, and kapow! It'll be like he just stuck his finger in a industrial strength light socket. He'll go down so fast he won't know what hit him.

"How many volts we talkin' about here?" Asked Dweeb.

"Not sure." Answered The Swede. "But I do know that it won't do any permanent damage to him. I just don't wanna be around him when he comes to. Hopefully we'll have him duct-taped to a chair by then, so he can settle down. We'll have to keep him secured until Carmen can get packed up and moved out of the county."

It was a drastic plan, but we'd seen how Spam reacts to his hoof-mug. Drastic situations demand drastic measures. We sat around and waited. The wait wasn't long.

It started out as a low rumble, slowly building to a deafening roar. Actually, that's exactly what it was; Spam roaring. It had the definite strains of a mating water-buffalo. Soon, Spam came into view. He was hurtling along with all the purpose of a road-grater; but a road-grater with a funny-car, nitro-injected engine. We formed a human wall in front of Carmen's trailer, hoping we could slow down his progress, knowing full well that we had as much chance as a child's sand-castle in the path of a tidal-wave.

We'd also arranged whatever obstacles were laying around in Carmen's yard directly in the path of the front door, in case he got past us.

Two seconds later he got past us.

By the time we'd come to our senses, Spam was trying his best to lift the rusted-out, '57 Chevy that was blocking the steps to the trailer. No surprise to us, he was making pretty good headway. We figured things couldn't get any worse. I was mistaken. About the time that Spam, the irresistible force, was trying to lift the immovable Chevy, Carmen walked out onto the porch to see what all the ruckus was about. We couldn't believe our foul luck; while she stood there taking in the sights, she took a big swig out of Spam's hoof-mug. It was right about that time that Spam went well beyond nuts, clean through freaked-out, and completely beyond warp factor five.

Spam officially went postal.

In a feat of strength that I wish I could've gotten on tape, making me immeasurable amounts of money from one of those TV shows that look for that type of stuff, Spam actually lifted the '57 Chevy like it was, oh, I don't know, maybe a Vega hatch-back, and tossed it aside. Luckily for us, and for Carmen, who was watching the spectacle with a sort of detached bemusement, The Swede had regained enough of his brain-cells to get him heading in Spam's general direction. With one mighty leap, The Swede flew through the air, the Tazer outstretched, and planted it firmly in the back of Spam's leg. It was like Spam was a puppet and his strings were cut. Gravity took over in record time and the Spamster dropped like a sack of spam.

In a flash, the rest of us were over there, madly wrapping the duct-tape around him while Dweeb raced Carmen inside and started hastily throwing her stuff into a suitcase and escorting her to the nearest airport for the first flight to Bora-Bora.

Thirty seconds later Spam started coming around. It didn't take him long to realize our treachery and he began madly thrashing. After about twelve minutes of thrashing he ran out of adrenaline and finally keeled over on his side. We got him home, but didn't figure it would be safe to unwrap him for a few hours. After explaining to him, in detail, why we did what we did, and showing him that the hoof-mug was safely back where it belonged, he agreed not to kill all of us with an assortment of garden implements.

Thus, the reason Spam was speechless when I threw Carmen the Klepto at him. Every guy has dated at least one PBFH at one time or another; Carmen just happened to be Spam's. I doubt he'll take any more shots at some of the women I've dated in the past.

"Okay, Bryan," jumped in Spam, "you got me on the Carmen bit. But what about that girl you were hangin' out with who kept saying she could seriously identify with Jeffery Dahmer?"

Nuts. I was hoping he'd forgotten that one.

26
The Man Who Said, *Yes*

It was a dark and stormy night.

All right, so I'm lying. It wasn't terribly dark or particularly stormy. This is Oregon, so I guess it was kind of grey and drizzly. So much for atmosphere.

It was night though, that much was true. A couple of my pals and I were huddled around a table at "Lloyd's Den of Inniquity," nursing our Spanish coffee's when my friend Otis Hamhand noticed a lone figure sitting quietly in the corner.

"Who's that?" Otis asked.

All eyes turned to the person in question. He was dressed in somber tones of brown and grey, a ragged collar pulled up around his weathered face to shelter it from prying eyes. He stared out onto the empty autumn streets, through watery eyes the color of slate. His face bore a languid look of peace that bordered on sadness; a face that had felt the brush-stroke of years filled with regret and remorse, etched deep with lines earned through misery. It was a face that reflected wishes yet unfulfilled.

If he was aware of our presence he didn't acknowledge it. Perhaps he was drawing on memories long since forgotten, because memories were the only possessions he now held.

"That, my friends, is 'The man who said, yes.' And for the price of a drink, he'll tell you his story."

I alone was the only person at the table who knew the tale of "The man who said, yes." Years earlier I'd seen him sitting at the end of a bar and by the end of the night had heard his sad story. It's a story all men should hear, because it could save them from a similar fate.

You wouldn't expect such sage advice to flow from this denizen of the streets, but wisdom often comes from the most unlikely sources. He had earned his knowledge through bitter mistakes, but could at least take solace in knowing that the fruits of his misery may benefit others.

I took them over to the man's table. "Excuse me, but my friends would like to hear your tale."

At first it was as if he didn't hear me. He continued to stare out onto the streets. Finally, he raised a weathered hand, snapped his fingers twice and called out to the bartender. "Bourbon. Rocks. Make it a double."

The bartender poured the man's drink and set in down reverently before him. The man reached over, grasped the shot glass and, in one fluid motion, downed the whiskey.

He then slowly turned to face us all. And when he spoke, you could have heard a pin drop. "So, you want to hear of my misery, do you?" The voice was deep and resonant, a voice that may have once carried authority, but now only drew pity.

"I was a man once. I held a responsible job, I made good money, I had my own home. That was, of course, before my. . .ah, error in judgement. Before I said, *yes"*

Everyone hung on his every word. There was the feeling that some great mystery was about to be exposed; brought forth out of the swirling mists of time.

"I was handsome, popular. Women adored me!" He then turned his eyes back to the streets. "That is, before I commited, what I like to call *'single-man's heresy.'"*

He motioned for us all to sit around his table as he continued the tale. He pointed a clawed hook of a finger at Otis, "You there, let me ask you this. If your girlfriend got a new haircut; something absolutely attrocious, and she asked if you liked it, what would you say?"

Otis didn't blink an eye. "I'd say, 'You bet honey! Looks great!'"

The old man grinned a sly, all-knowing grin. "Of course you would."

He then turned to Dweeb, sitting to my left. "And you! If you girlfriend was utterly flat-chested and asked if you wish she had boobs like Claudia Schiffer, what would you say?"

Dweeb also never gave it a thought. He'd read his *guy handbook*. "I'd tell her she was great just the way she was."

The old man just smiled some more. "In other words, you'd lie your pants off."

We all looked around the table and nodded our agreement. "Sure. You betcha. In a heartbeat. Not a question."

The old man's grin slowly melted from his face. "That's what I used to do, too. But then, I decided to try something different; something radical. I decided I'd see what would happen if I gave truthful answers; to see what would happen if I said, *yes.*

His voice went suddenly quiet, as his eyes took on a soft, distant look. "What was I thinking?"

His words slowly sank in around the table. The looks on my friends faces spoke volumes. They looked around at one another, hardly believing what they'd just heard. Finally Otis could no longer contain his disbelief.

"You answered truthfully?"

"You actually said, *yes?*" Chimed in Dweeb.

The old man wasn't offended. He'd heard these remarks many, many times over the years. "Sadly, it's true. I still remember that fateful day. My girlfriend Felicia had been gaining weight in leaps and bounds, but like a good guy, I didn't say anything. Finally, though, she asked the question that would forever change my life. She asked me if I thought she was getting fat. I figured, what the hell, we've been dating for a while. She can take the truth. I said. . .'As a matter of fact, *yes.*'

"I still remember the stillness that followed. She couldn't believe her ears. She'd been around enough to know that guys are supposed to lie in those situations. They know we're lying, but they don't care. They just want us to tell them they still have the Barbie doll figure they had five sizes ago.

"If I could have stopped time, rolled back the clock and never uttered that cursed word, I would have. One word, one syllable, and my life began a long miserable spiral into the abyss."

The old man continued. "And it didn't take long for word to spread. You know how women talk."

Everyone nodded at this painful truth.

"Before I knew it, I couldn't get a date. Women refused to return my phone calls. I was spurned, an outcast. I was a leper among the clean. It was only a matter of time before all I had built came crashing down around me."

Otis reached for a napkin to dab at his eyes. Dweeb was so choked up he could hardly finish his beer.

"I began losing clients. . .word was out! Every time I would enter a room, conversations would abruptly come to an end." The old man clenched and reclenched his fists at the obviously painful memories he was dredging up. "The withering stares, the looks of disapproval. I had to have my phone number unlisted after the torrent of threats I received. After one particularly nasty message I used my call-return service to find out who'd seen fit to abuse me so vigorously. The number was traced to a convent! I was getting death threats from nuns! It was at this point I realized that even God wasn't on my side and I retreated from the world I'd once embraced."

No one at the table could look him in the eye. It was a difficult story to listen to, all the more because we knew that he deserved everything he got.

"I lost my job, my family disowned me. Even my dog ran away. Whenever people passed me on the streets I could hear their whispers to one another. . . 'Look, isn't that the man who said, *yes*?' I'd reached the bottom. All as a result of a single syllable."

His story was finished. The old man leaned back and took a deep breath in an effort to compose himself again.

Otis was the first to speak. "You old fool! Do you expect our pity? You've read the *handbook*! It specifically points out that under no circumstances are you to give an honest response to a potentially hazardous question! They should update the *handbook* with your pathetic story as a warning to what can happen when you try to get cute, and go against time-honored rules."

"Settle down, Otis," I gently admonished, "he's paid for his mistakes."

"That's right, son." said the old man, "I've paid my pound of flesh. My only hope is that maybe if enough men hear my story no one else will ever try to buck the system again."

"Yeah," said Otis, "I suppose you've suffered enough. And don't you worry, my buddies and I will never, ever tell the truth if our girlfriends ask us if we think they're getting fat. You can count on it."

The old man just smiled.